CARVING CLASSICAL STYLES IN WOOD

CARVING CLASSICAL STYLES IN WOOD

FREDERICK WILBUR

GUILD OF MASTER CRAFTSMAN PUBLICATIONS LTD

First published 2004 by
Guild of Master Craftsman Publications Ltd
Castle Place, 166 High Street,
Lewes, East Sussex BN7 1XU

Reprinted 2006

ISBN-13: 978-1-86108-363-0
ISBN-10: 1-86108-363-7

A catalogue record for this book is available from the British Library.

Managing Editor: Gerrie Purcell
Production Manager: Hilary MacCullum
Editor: Stephen Haynes
Book and cover design: Ian Hunt Design
Photographs and drawings are by the author except where
otherwise stated.

Set in Albertina and Helvetica

Color origination by Icon Reproduction
Printed and bound by Kyodo Printing (Singapore)

SAFETY

Woodcarving should not be a dangerous activity, provided that sensible precautions are taken to avoid unnecessary risk.

- Always ensure that work is securely held in a suitable clamp or other device, and that the workplace lighting is adequate.

- Keep tools sharp; blunt tools are dangerous because they require more pressure and may behave unpredictably. Store them so that you, and others, cannot touch their cutting edges accidentally.

- Be particular about disposing of shavings, finishing materials, oily rags, etc., which may be a fire hazard.

- Do not work when your concentration is impaired by drugs, alcohol, or fatigue.

- Do not remove safety guards from power tools; pay attention to electrical safety.

- It is not safe to use a chainsaw without the protective clothing which is specially designed for this purpose, and attendance on a recognized training course is strongly recommended. Be aware that regulations governing chainsaw use are revised from time to time.

The safety advice in this book is intended for your guidance, but cannot cover every eventuality: the safe use of hand and power tools is the responsibility of the user. If you are unhappy with a particular technique or procedure, do not use it—there is always another way.

Measurements
Although care has been taken to ensure that the metric measurements are true and accurate, they are only conversions from imperial; they have been rounded up or down to the nearest whole millimeter, or to the nearest convenient equivalent in cases where the imperial measurements themselves are only approximate. When following the projects, use either the metric or the imperial measurements; do not mix units.

This book is dedicated to my
granddaughter
Cailin
and a new generation of woodcarvers

A Small Wonder

As I work in the quiet of my shop
Carving mahogany into the likeness
  Of a bird,
I notice an echo of my efforts
And pause, putting down gouge and strop,
To discover what creature distracts me
  Though barely heard.

A house wren scratches among cans of motor oil,
Chrome spout, and blue windshield wash
  In a tangle
Of moss she has gleaned from woods nearby.
Impressed with her patient toil,
I observe her pregnant purpose,
How her fussy flit and wrangle

Fabricate an artful nest. For such intention
(Chips molted willy-nilly)
  I can only hope.
I return to my work flustered,
Eyeing the grain. It is a feeble rendition
Of the flying fancy—a dream
  Beyond my skill and scope.

ACKNOWLEDGMENTS

In a spirit of humbled gratitude, I would like to acknowledge all the clients who have had faith and confidence in my work over the years. Without their repeated commissions, I would not have been able to practice my craft—certainly not to make a living by it—or to write this book.

I want to thank my wife, Elizabeth, who continues to support my efforts with amazing patience, enthusiastic encouragement, and thoughtful criticism.

I also want to express a special appreciation to Stephen Haynes, my editor, whose patience, kind words, and editorial expertise have contributed immensely to the enjoyment of producing this book.

Many others have assisted me in various ways:

Anita Ellis, Director of Curatorial Affairs; Ted Lind, Curator of Education; Scott Hisey, Photographic Coordinator/Rights and Reproductions Administrator, Cincinnati Art Museum.

Amy Miller Dehan, Assistant Director of Curatorial Affairs at the Cincinnati Art Museum, whom I would especially like to thank for her hospitality, interest, and enthusiasm during and since my visit to Cincinnati.

John Grafton for permission to reproduce illustrations from several works published by Dover Publications Inc.

John Lavine, Editor of *Woodwork*, and Ross Periodicals for the use of an article of my authorship (#72, February 2002).

GMC Publications Ltd for the use of an article of my authorship in *Woodcarving* (#41, May/June 1998).

Todd D. Prickett of C. L. Prickett for the photograph of the Philadelphia lowboy.

Jean Pey of the Musée Archéologique, Nîmes, France for the photographs of the Maison Carrée.

Terry Byrd Eason for the use of his design for the liturgical chair fan, and Peter Brown, Pastor of First Presbyterian Church, Rocky Mount, NC, for permission to photograph the chair.

Steve and Chloe Raynor for permitting photography of their mantelpiece with sunburst carvings.

Tracy Bomento, Rights and Permissions, Philadelphia Museum of Art.

Francesco Buranelli of Monumenti, Musei e Gallerie Pontificie (Vatican Museums).

Roberta G. Laynor, Architectural Conservator and Keeper of the Francis H. Lenygon Collection of Architectural Fragments at the Colonial Williamsburg Foundation.

Phillip Beaurline for photography.

Howell W. Perkins, Manager, Department of Photographic Resources, Virginia Museum of Fine Art.

Kevin Maxson and Jessica Wilbur for photography and research.

Mark A. Collins for the use of his watercolor *Legacy*.

Virginia Metalcrafters Inc. for the use of the pattern of the Christmas wreath.

Victor Deupi and Carroll W. Westfall of the University of Notre Dame School of Architecture for inviting me to participate in the Spring Lecture Series 2000.

CONTENTS

INTRODUCTION

The woodcarving trade • The need for custom work

For woodcarvers and those interested in classical ornament, this book addresses many elements of the classical style as applied to architecture and the decoration of furniture. The approach is similar to my previous book, *Carving Architectural Detail in Wood: The Classical Tradition* (GMC Publications, 2000), in which I discussed the origins of classical architecture, its use of proportion, the orders, and the most prominent elements of ornamentation, including mouldings, volutes, rosettes, and capitals. My intention in this work is to build on that foundation by examining and demonstrating additional elements associated with classical design.

The woodcarving in this book is based on the enduring tenets of classicism as they have been modified and revived through time—what is often called classical "style". Enthusiasts would argue that classicism is not a transient style, but an archetypal world-view. Instead of reiterating the basic definitions of classicism, Chapter 1 addresses some of these issues. This chapter is not intended to be exhaustive, either in terms of historical examples or philosophical points of view, but to make the woodcarver aware of different interpretations within the idiom of classicism and to point out the differences in style which can be observed. The emphasis, of course, is on carved wood ornamentation, though I have included examples in stone which could legitimately be imitated in wood. What may appear to be gross generalizations to scholars will serve to guide the woodcarver, millwork (joinery) specifier, and architect in the direction of understanding the proper terminology and the characteristics of period styles. Throughout the book, these comments are supplemented by photographs of a number of variations. The primary concern of this book, however, is to explain in words and sequence photographs how to carve some pervasive elements, such as the cartouche, the shell, the keystone, and the finial. The concluding chapter brings these elements together in some suggested applications.

> *Perhaps ornament has been such a consistent part of human history because it has satisfied a need for beauty that all people share.*
>
> BRENT C. BROLIN,
> *ARCHITECTURAL ORNAMENT: BANISHMENT AND RETURN*

THE WOODCARVING TRADE TODAY

In recent years there has been an increased interest in classical architecture and ornament among architects, designers, and a sophisticated clientele. This is evident in a number of areas: the plethora of periodicals and publications devoted to classical style, television programs addressing restoration and historic detail, and the continued construction of buildings using the classical vocabulary. To further this interest there are efforts to educate architectural and millwork professionals, as well as the general public, by organizations such as the Architectural Woodwork Institute and the Institute of Classical Architecture & Classical America. In response to the demand for classical ornament, there is a growing number of young people pursuing architectural woodcarving as a viable livelihood. Woodcarving, more generally, is currently enjoying a renaissance, with active organizations such as the National Wood Carvers Association in America and the British Woodcarvers Association in the UK.

Questions about how to get started in the trade appear frequently in the woodcarving periodicals. Several articles have been written on this subject, but few address the practical aspects of running a business. Mostly, readers are concerned with where to learn the trade, with the extent of their talent, and whether one can earn a living while learning. Some ask about pricing, but curiosity about business practices is rare.

Information about the artistic and business background, aspirations, and resources of the prospective carver is required in order to answer these questions thoroughly. Leaving aside the controversy of apprenticeship versus being self-taught, one will learn regardless, if strongly motivated to do so. There are many schools and teachers with a lot to offer, though taking advantage of them may be difficult for some. There are, in addition, many good resource and instruction books available from which to learn the art. As in any endeavor of this nature, self-discipline, patience, and curiosity are the main requirements.

Talent is one of those slippery concepts which get mixed up with the largely discredited dichotomy of art versus craft. One should pursue what is of interest, exciting, and enjoyable. Procuring a decent living depends on more than "talent". It is not uncommon to find an extremely talented person who just can't get organized, make money, or be happy. Don't worry about talent.

It is obvious to me that one needs to have some experience, to have a "track record", before setting up as a full-time business. This is not to say that one has to be a master carver—the true artisan is continually learning. After 25 years earning a living by woodcarving, I still learn from others, still experiment (sometimes disastrously), still nick my finger from time to time. Success is a combination of many different talents.

THE BUSINESS OF CARVING

The purpose, facilities, and approach of the trade carver are not so different from those of other artisans, such as a stained-glass artist supplying glazing for an entry door or a blacksmith forging custom hinges for an Arts and Crafts cabinet. Though the present-day carver occasionally has assistants, he or she usually works alone; the large carving shop is rare. This means that the carver wears all the hats (and all the Band-aids®!), being the receptionist, the sales department, the draftsman, specifier, and estimator; the tool maintenance guy, purchasing agent, gofer, janitor, and when there is time, a woodcarver. The carver may have a variety of interests, whether in academic issues or in practical aspects of the building trades, but in any case there is a desire for manual activity. Invariably, carvers obtain their skill from years of practice. Though some

may have art training, or have served apprenticeships, ultimately each of us is self-taught because success depends upon practice.

To have a successful business it is absolutely necessary to be self-disciplined. Without attention to business as well as artistic details, one will have a hard time creating a viable business. One must be willing to devote time and energy to the business; as Thomas Edison said, "Genius is 10% inspiration and 90% perspiration."

Most artists do not have a background in business when they begin their careers. At best they may have jotted down a few figures which passed as a business plan. There is an abundance of self-help books on the subject, which all stress that one should think realistically about a future business. To establish a clear idea of the purpose of the business in concrete as well as idealistic terms, one should consider such questions as: what will be the usual overhead expenses, the anticipated income, and most importantly, who will buy the product? Unless one has capital for start-up and for sustaining the business for a while, developing a transition plan will be necessary. It is advantageous to accumulate basic tools and equipment and a few "side" jobs before chucking the 9 to 5 job. Keeping track of the time spent on these jobs will give one a more realistic sense of how much to charge per hour.

Most artisans consistently work long hours and weekends, do their office work in the evenings, and are not indulgent vacationers. One has to be realistic about expectations in terms of lifestyle. (Of course, everyone's financial situation and obligations are different.) Many survive by maintaining low overhead costs, little debt, and few financial commitments; in other words, by adopting a fiscally responsible approach. For an individual craftsman, there is not a lot of financial buffer between proud profit, sneaking by, and utter discouragement.

Most carvers work in very modest environments: basements, sheds, and garages. I am fortunate to work in a shop of a little over 1000 sq ft ($93m^2$)—a converted three-car garage with addition. The carving room (Fig 0.1) has a high ceiling, with sets of lights on different switches and lots of windows. The benches, gouge storage, and sharpening station are arranged in close proximity to each other. I have a modestly equipped machine room. But the fanciest shop and equipment don't make a successful business: one has to understand the niche one's product or service occupies in the marketplace.

In simple terms, there are two approaches to marketing: to make a product and then sell it to the customer (retail), or to have clients come to you to have work

Fig 0.1 *A general view of my well-lit carving room*

done (commission). There are, of course, advantages and drawbacks to either modus operandi. It probably boils down to your own personality, and how you like to do things and interact with people. A woodcarving for the retail market has to be produced inexpensively (until you become well known, at least), which means that quite a few items have to be made efficiently.

I think of carving by commission as a service, and not as the manufacture of a product. In a sense, trade carvers don't produce anything, but beautify everything. Indeed, they often give back less than they receive, having chipped away a wheelbarrow full of wood! What they are selling is their knowledge and skill. The biggest disadvantage of working to commission is that often the design aspects are predetermined by client, architect, or other designer. Also, because commission carvers are usually considered subcontractors by the millwork or furniture company, the decorative carvings they are asked to produce are but bits and pieces of larger construction projects—so they usually do not see their carvings with finish, in context, or installed. They are at the bottom of the totem pole, so to speak. But I do not disparage; the greatest works of Western art were done to commission.

As a subcontractor, I ask that the material be supplied dimensioned, profiled, and ready to carve. This saves a lot of machine time; after all, I would rather be carving. The key to woodcarving, indeed to any craft, is in understanding the intended outcome, knowing the appropriate method, and performing operations in sequence. Don't worry: there is plenty of personal involvement and creative design, despite the drudgery of jobs requiring repetitive multiples.

THE DEMAND FOR CUSTOM WORK

One may wonder why there is a market these days for architectural woodcarving at all, but there are many woodworking and architectural situations requiring the expertise of the decorative woodcarver.

- Hand-shaping is sometimes needed for seemingly mundane geometric pieces. These items are impractical or impossible to accomplish on conventional machinery because of tight radii, compound curves, acute corners, or diminishing profiles. Examples include compound-curved handrails, stopped reeds

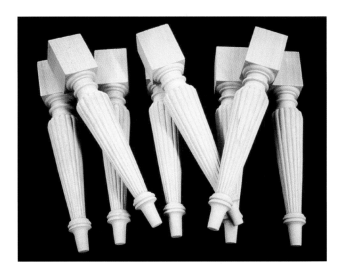

Fig 0.2 *These neoclassical table legs require hand-carving, because the tapered reeds "die" top and bottom into other elements*

13

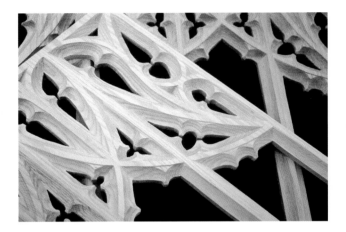

Fig 0.3 Gothic tracery is a staple of the ecclesiastical woodcarver

Fig 0.5 A substantial batch of hand-carved Ionic capitals

(as in the table legs of Fig 0.2), Gothic tracery (Fig 0.3), and the diminishing astragal-and-cyma profile of keystones (discussed in Chapter 5).

- Not all handwork is one-of-a-kind: sometimes the carver is asked to produce small quantities of an item which *could* be fabricated by mechanical or computer-assisted means, except that it is impractical or too expensive to do so. This sort of commission might include sets of drapery swags (Fig 0.4), column capitals (Fig 0.5), or many other elements, made in batches from just a few to a few dozen.

- One of the more obvious occasions for the carver's labor is the need to replicate missing elements in the renovation or restoration of older structures or antique (and sometimes not so antique) furniture. The fireplace backband in Fig 0.6 is from Blandfield, a Tidewater Virginia house built in 1769 and restored

in the 1980s. The scrolled brackets in Fig 0.7 were made for Foley Square Courthouse in New York.

- The carver is often called upon to furnish items of a specific dimension which are unavailable elsewhere; this includes console brackets, finials, rosettes, capitals, and many other elements. Moulding is a good example (Fig 0.8). As the millworker should know, in quality woodwork the design elements need to be seamlessly integrated, both literally and aesthetically. An illustration of this point is prefabricated egg-and-dart moulding, which is nearly impossible to miter without causing discontinuity of design and grotesquely mismatched "eggs". The traditional way (derived from the ancient Greeks) to deal with this difficulty is to carve a leaf at the miter joint so that the egg-and-dart appears to run underneath it (Fig 0.9). To do this, of course, requires that the lengths of moulding be fitted together prior to carving them.

Fig 0.4 Swags of drapery may be carved by hand if it is uneconomical to reproduce them mechanically

Fig 0.6 Detail of a fireplace at Blandfield, VA, carved by the author in the 1980s

Fig 0.7 *A pair of console brackets made by the author for a restoration project*

Fig 0.8 *Repeated lengths of moulding may need to be carved by hand to fit a particular space*

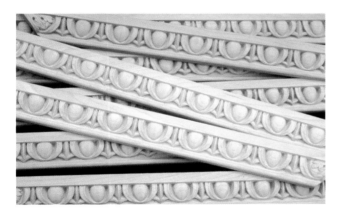

Fig 0.9 *Hand-carved leaves are the accepted way of negotiating miter joints in egg-and-dart moulding*

- The carver's services are also needed when off-the-shelf products are not of the desired wood species. In many instances it doesn't matter which species of wood is used, as paint may be the finish. In others, it matters for practical or aesthetic reasons: basswood (*Tilia americana*), for instance, does not sustain wear

well, so it is not used for doorjambs. Or there may be stylistic reasons: Gothic church work and Tudor linenfold panels are historically of oak (*Quercus* spp.); Chippendale chairs are mahogany (*Swietenia* spp.). From a carver's point of view, material with little figure is preferable because the sculptural form is what is important; jazzy grain patterns would only distract the viewer. The rosettes in Fig 0.10, carved in sassafras (*Sassafras albidum*), look very much like oak but are softer and lighter in weight. The orchids carved on the legs of a coffee table (Fig 0.11) are of

Fig 0.10 *Sassafras is substituted for oak in these oval rosettes*

Fig 0.11 *The carvings on these coffee-table legs represent orchids indigenous to Africa*

Fig 0.12 Carved oak altarpiece by the author, Grace and Holy Trinity Cathedral, Kansas City, MO

Fig 0.13 Coat of arms carved by the author

Fig 0.14 Hand-carved pattern for a decorative brass casting

shedua or ovangkol (*Guibourtia ehie*). The reredos at Grace and Holy Trinity Cathedral, Kansas City, MO (Fig 0.12), is white oak (*Quercus alba*).

- Many carvers design and letter signs for individuals and businesses, incorporating pictorials, fancy calligraphy, and corporate logos. Among these wood graphics are heraldic coats of arms (Fig 0.13), seals, and insignia, for individuals as well as educational and governmental institutions. I began my carving career by making signs, and I suspect others have as well.

- There is some call for carvers to produce models—or, more properly, patterns—for industry. Some are for reproduction in plaster and concrete, while others are for foundries. The wreath in Fig 0.14 is a model for a brass Christmas stocking hanger produced by Virginia Metalcrafters, Inc. after an example made for Colonial Williamsburg.

- The custom carver is in a position to oblige the personal sensibility of the individual client who wants and can afford a unique piece of art. Often this is the occasion for the carver to be creative and promote his or her own "style". A frequent request is for a mantelpiece, either with indigenous flora and fauna or with more classical acanthus foliage. Other common projects include an array of household items such as cabinet and entry doors, picture and mirror frames,

Fig 0.15 Floral panel designed and carved by the author

Fig 0.16 (Left) Projects such as this candlestick combine carving with simple woodturning

Fig 0.17 (Above) Pineapple finials are discussed in detail in Chapter 6

and candlesticks. Pictured in Fig 0.15 is a floral door panel for a kitchen. Of course, decorative sculptures and relief panels are also included in this category.

- Often the carver must develop skills in other areas in order to produce a more complete piece. These may include woodturning and gilding, two areas in which I am modestly proficient. By producing my own blanks for finials, urns, candlesticks (Fig 0.16), balusters, table legs, and pineapples (Fig 0.17), I can be more efficient and have more control over the quality than when the work is subcontracted to a professional turner. Finishing, painting, and the ability to lay gold leaf are often required, as much sign lettering and many architectural elements, especially in ecclesiastical work, are polychromed and gilded (Fig 0.18).

- Not least, the carver collaborates with furniture makers and interior decorators to embellish pieces of furniture such as the Gothic bench in Fig 0.19, or accessory items like the Gothic coffer in Fig 0.20. Having a wide background in historical ornament gives one the versatility to take on both traditional styles and those of a more modern nature.

Fig 0.18 An example of ecclesiastical carving by the author, painted and gilded

Fig 0.19 Gothic-style carving on a replica of a church bench

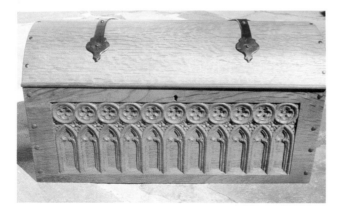

Fig 0.20 Gothic arcading on an otherwise plain oak coffer

HANDLING A COMMISSION

The hardest tasks for most artisans are timekeeping and accurate cost estimating. These, of course, are directly related. Over the years I have worked out a simple system of transferring the recorded data from a time sheet to a listing which itemizes each element. So, when a quotation is requested for a Corinthian capital, for instance, I can turn to the listing of all my past jobs which involved Corinthian capitals. Though each job is different in one aspect or another, I can then arrive at a fair estimate, based on experience.

And over time, the artisan can anticipate more clearly the potential complications of a job, both physically and "politically". Also over time, one becomes more committed to maintaining the highest personal standard and less willing to compromise that standard to meet a deadline. This does not mean that pressure is eliminated; the successful artisan generally has a backlog of several months, with a dozen or so estimates pending at any given time.

Often the carver is asked to design the required element. For an architectural carver there is a need to combine mechanical and freehand drawing. The information provided may include a verbal description, but this is rare. Drawings are often scribbled, partly smudged, without dimensions, section views, or any other indication that they are not doodles of an eighth-grader. Increasingly these days one receives crisp, computer-generated drawings, but unfortunately these do not represent carved elements accurately or with any of the sensibility required of the carver. What appears to be a neat Art Deco capital turns out instead to represent a poorly rendered Corinthian capital. Even some book illustrations, where shading has been applied in a mechanical way, tend to flatten and homogenize the subtleties of the third dimension—one misses the sense of daylight changing.

When offered a commission, the first task is to review the material and determine the customer's basic intentions. If both photographs and drawings are supplied, compare the two for congruence; don't assume the designer understands what he draws. What is being represented? What are the dimensions? Is the information accurate and consistent? What is the material? Does grain orientation matter? If it is other than a solid block of wood, how will it be fabricated? What is the installed context? And this is before we come to aesthetic questions. How literally should the design be interpreted? How much relief is intended? What is the style? What will be the lighting situation? The whole process is made up of questions; even in the carving itself, decisions are constantly being made. Usually calls have to be made to prospective clients to clarify some point and, in some extreme situations, help them understand the complexities involved and ultimately find common ground in differing terminology. Whether drawings are supplied or pages are ripped from magazines, a full-size drawing will be needed. It is sometimes curious, but always clarifying, to see how large something is in the shop when it fits so neatly on a piece of paper. I often redraw the design to help my own understanding of the project.

I then arrive at a cost estimate, taking into consideration by whom or in what manner the blank will be produced (the *material*), and then the *time* needed for the actual carving of the piece. Factors such as the wood species, the amount of relief desired, the detail, the overall size, all contribute to the estimation of time. When communicating with the client, I correlate the price with the item as represented by the drawing. I include a contract delineating the responsibilities of both parties. This addresses copyright ownership, the use of photographs, and payment for samples. Specifications include materials, and sometimes carving details such as depth of relief, surface texture, and finish. The drawing upon which the cost quotation is based becomes part of the contract. Practical aspects such as shipping costs, retainers, and payment schedules as well as liability issues are also spelled out. Consult an up-to-date reference book for further information on contracts.

I approach my work as I am sure most carvers do: as an artist as well as an artisan, and in a spirit of practicality, self-discipline, and mindfulness. The idea of making something by hand and eye , and the notion that there is nothing inherently wrong with imperfection, lend dignity to manual labor and value to human endeavor. Each piece of handwork embodies a story, a tale of process, and a personal commitment by the maker. A carving may well have irregularities, design flaws, or other oddities; we call such things "character". But craftsmanship involves sensitivity to materials, design, and the tools of the trade, a striving for perfection, confidence, and peace.

When I look closely at an old carving, I note the telltale signs of human idiosyncrasy and understand the technique, intention, and a smidgen of the man or woman who put gouge to wood. Though there are many machine-carved products on the market, they do not show the mark of the maker. And that's the main reason carvers do what they do. We are lucky to be able to make a living doing what we enjoy.

When the work is done, I put it back in the box and send it to the millwork or furniture company, never to see it again. Sometimes it is a disheartening experience, with only photographs to show for it; sometimes it is a relief to have concluded the job. In any event, I hope that the client is tickled with what I've done, whether a traditional design with a several-thousand-year pedigree or something more tentative from my own vision.

A NOTE ON TERMINOLOGY

Throughout this book the following terms have consistently been used as defined below:

blank a piece of material which has been shaped by hand or machine to the dimensions of the element to be made, such as a lathe-turned rosette, shaper-run moulding, or the complex curves of a Corinthian capital produced by large gouges and files.

design the two-dimensional drawing or cartoon of the ornament to be made.

grounding the background: either the recessed part of the blank, or the surface upon which the ornamentation is applied.

layout the process of using the pattern, as well as other guidelines, to define the shape of the carved element on the blank.

modeling the surface treatment carried out after the outline of the ornamentation has been defined.

pattern any means of transferring the design to the material, such as a photocopied drawing glued onto the blank, a tracing, or a metal template.

profile the sectional shape of an element—usually in referring to mouldings which have been formed with shaped cutters.

Other terms printed in bold type in the text are defined in the Glossary.

Note that tool numbers cited in the text are those used by Pfeil of Switzerland, unless otherwise stated.

Some of the material in this chapter is from a talk given at the University of Notre Dame School of Architecture in the spring of 2000, and subsequently published in Woodwork *magazine, #72 (February 2002).*

CLASSICAL STYLES

Idiom and style • Principles of design

I hesitated to use the word "style" in the title of this book, because its meaning can be burdened with paralyzing complexity. Many serious classicists would argue that there are no classical styles, only variations on a theme. It is an area of study which can be addressed from a number of perspectives. One may consider it in terms of design principles, changing ideas of beauty, functional aspects, or consequences of manufacture; or in terms of the cultural interactions of economics, politics, and religion. There are differing opinions about meaning and function, form and content; and, of course, there are controversies involving historical interpretation. The academic arguments do not concern us here. For the architectural woodcarver, the objective is to replicate classical motifs accurately or to design historically "correct" ones in a sensitive but practical manner.

With the increased economic viability of traditional crafts in recent years, and with the public becoming more educated about classical architecture, it is incumbent upon the present-day carver to be familiar with the salient features of "classical style". Novice architectural carvers may have the notion that they must develop their own style, but it is my feeling that only by understanding historical precedent, and proficiently executing those styles, can we arrive at our own "vision" in a meaningful way.

Style is usually identified by outward or obvious details within an overall framework or **idiom**. For our purposes, style is a distinctive quality of artistic expression which characterizes a cultural group within a given time period. This definition does not address individual styles or radically transient "fashion" except in a few rare

> *Ornament corresponds to the highest category of building, beauty; and, because it is artificial, ornament outdoes nature.*
>
> KATHLEEN WEIL-GARRIS BRANDT (PARAPHRASING LEON BATTISTA ALBERTI)

cases, such as "Adam style". The distinction implies a larger cultural or historical context, and this is especially so when discussing classical ornament. (It is particularly apt that the Greek antecedent *stylos* means "pillar", because classical architecture, almost without exception, features columns.)

Many analogies could be used to explain the relationship between idiom and style; let us use poetry. The styles of a Shakespearean sonnet and the free verse of Allen Ginsberg seem quite different, but both satisfy the criteria which make them poetry: namely, attention to line length, the heightened use of sound, the employment of rhythm, and the compression of meaning. Architectural style relies on the underlying idiom for expressions of form, function, and appropriate ornament. Though form is important to both the poetic styles mentioned above, they are radically different in style. It is the variation within the idiom which distinguishes the two poems, or two classical styles. One might say that style is in the details.

If we compare the building façades of Figs 1.1–1.8, we can readily understand the concept of varying styles within a coherent idiom. Each example has columns, an entablature, and a pediment, and embodies the principles of symmetry and proportion, even though the examples are drawn from a lengthy time span. Yet each is stylistically different. The United States Supreme Court building of 1935 (Fig 1.1) is a literal translation of the classical temple, as is the eighteenth-century Temple of Aesculapius in the grounds of the Villa Borghese (Fig 1.2). They both resemble the Maison Carrée, a Roman temple of 16 BCE (Fig 1.3). The façade of St Peter's, built between 1506 and

Fig 1.1 (Above) *US Supreme Court building, Washington, DC*

Fig 1.2 (Right) *Temple of Aesculapius, in the grounds of the Villa Borghese, Rome*

Fig 1.3 (Below) *Maison Carrée, Nîmes, France*

Fig 1.4 St Peter's basilica, Rome

Fig 1.5 Santa Susanna, Rome

Fig 1.6 St Martin-in-the-Fields, London

Fig 1.7 Villa Almerico, Vicenza, Italy

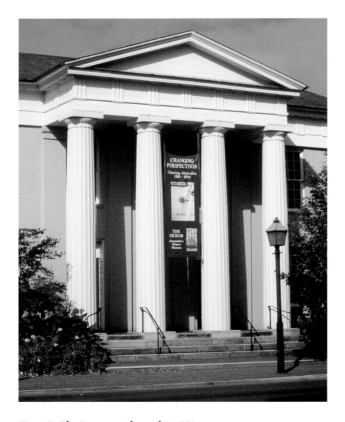

Fig 1.8 The Lyceum, Alexandria, VA

1626 (Fig 1.4), echoes this configuration and shares the sturdy horizontal orientation of the classical temple, but there are obvious alterations: to name only two, the pediment is reduced in prominence and the columns appear to be decorative instead of structural. Santa Susanna (façade built 1597–1603) again features classical elements, but emphasizes the vertical, stacking, as it were, two temple fronts on top of each other (Fig 1.5). St Martin-in-the-Fields (1722–6) has a fairly literal temple front, but also achieves verticality with the unclassical addition of a steeple (Fig 1.6). This church style was and continues to be a popular one in America.

As much as there has been a straying from the buildings of antiquity, there has been a rejuvenation of the idiom. The Villa Almerico of 1567 (Fig 1.7) is a powerful statement of symmetry, all four façades being repetitions of the same temple front. With the discovery and excavation of Pompeii, Herculaneum, and other ancient sites in the eighteenth century and the subsequent publication of "artifacts", the desire to reproduce authentic objects, ornamentation, and buildings spurred neoclassicism and the nineteenth-century Greek Revival. The Lyceum in Alexandria, Virginia (1839) is only one of hundreds of neoclassical buildings in America (Fig 1.8).

The general term **ornament** refers to the motif depicted—the thing itself, such as a lion's head, without context. **Decoration**, on the other hand, is the embellishment or enrichment of an object, such as a cartouche, keystone, or medallion with a lion's head applied to it. Thus, the decorated object can embody various ornaments, just as a poem may contain various figures of speech combined or juxtaposed. One illustration from classical architecture is the Ionic capital, which, though a functional form, is also a decorated element. The Greek version shown in Fig 1.9 (see also Fig 6.3 on page 120) is a nineteenth-century copy of those on the Erechtheion in Athens. It has a beaded astragal, an egg-and-dart echinus, volutes, balusters with leaves, and an abacus with water-leaf ornamentation. The fillets or beads which make up the spirals in the Greek version separate in the area between the volutes, the bottom ones drooping down to the top of the echinus. The Roman Ionic capital (Fig 1.10) has a similar configuration, but the "rind" (as Alberti calls it) joining the volutes is straight, and the "channel"

Fig 1.9 Greek Ionic capital copied from the Erechtheion, Athens

Fig 1.10 Roman-style Ionic capital on an engaged column. The rind or channel in this example is infilled with foliage

Fig 1.11 *Renaissance pilaster capital with grotesque mask and volutes*

Fig 1.12 *Capitals with unorthodox volute orientation*

Fig 1.13 *Capital with sunflowers in place of volutes*

(as Palladio calls the cove) is recessed from the egg-and-dart echinus, making the latter more prominent. A number of different variants and derivatives can be compared in Figs 1.11–1.14. It is variations like these in the character of ornament which give the best indication of architectural styles.

The concept of style is complicated by differences in time and geography. Ideas and innovations travel quickly or slowly by turns, depending upon cultural environments: the interaction produced by conquest or peace, trade or isolation, by innovation or repression. As Henry David Thoreau pointed out: "We are inclined to think of all Romans who lived within five hundred years B.C. as *contemporaries* to each other. Yet Time moved at the same deliberate pace then as now."

Historical labels rarely do justice to a subject, originating as they do after the fact and often pejoratively; but they nonetheless help us understand the complexity of art and cultural history. The individual artisan can be pictured as a human being with a daily list of botched experiments, snafus, and satisfactions (if not ecstasies!), some of which, for whatever reason, happen to survive. To pigeonhole such people as representatives of a particular style seems a stupendous injustice to them, but it serves to put their work in a historical context, and in that sense allows them some measure of immortality. It is safe to say that a stylistically "pure" building is unlikely to exist; cultural history is never so neat. And few buildings continue serving the purpose for which they were built.

Fig 1.14 "Scamozzi" capitals, with volutes turned at a 45° angle on all four corners

THE CLASSICAL IDIOM

Classicism is a world view, a perception of life, which sees beauty in order. The Greeks, fascinated with mathematics, forms, and proportions, built temples which have an apparent clarity, balance, symmetry, and restraint. "When the Classical Greek fashioned something, he required of the form that it give the clearest possible expression of the object's particular function" (H. P. L'Orange, *Art Forms and Civic Life in the Late Roman Empire*, p. 9). As we saw in Figs 1.1–1.3, the emphasis is on the exterior of the building, both in its architectural details and in its decoration. In later periods the emphasis shifts to the interior, but the basic tenets of classicism remain.

Fundamental to understanding the structure and decoration of classical structures is a comprehension of the **orders**. What is meant by this term is the overall relationship of the parts to the whole, each part playing a proportional role in creating a harmonious structure. The term *orders* does not appear until the writings of the Renaissance, but Vitruvius (active 46–30 BCE) and even earlier writers were concerned about proportion and the proper use and relationship of the various structural and decorative elements. "The importance of the orders can not be overstated: they are the DNA of classical architecture, the core of the mnemonic system by which its forms evolved and were transmitted" (Mark Wilson Jones, *Principles of Roman Architecture*, p. 109). Sebastiano Serlio (1475–1554) in his posthumously published work of 1584 was the first to illustrate a comparison of the orders (Fig 1.15). There have been innumerable comparisons and explanations since, by writers such as Giacomo da Vignola (1507–73), Andrea Palladio (1508–80), Vincenzo Scamozzi (1552–1616), Claude Perrault (1613–88), James Gibbs (1682–1754), William Chambers (1723–96), and, in our own day, Robert Chitham. It is easy to see from this partial list the continuity of the academic exploration of the subject.

The architectural woodcarver today is commissioned to carve a wide range of classical elements. Some are copied directly from artifacts, while others are only reminiscent of authentic designs. The carver may be asked to make Ionic, Corinthian, and occasionally Composite capitals, egg-and-dart moulding, and a mythological beast here and there. Generally the Roman versions are requested because, in spite of the immensely popular Greek Revival of the nineteenth century (especially in America), the Roman tradition enjoyed wider dissemination via numerous Renaissance and later writers: chiefly Palladio, the English Palladians, and Thomas Jefferson.

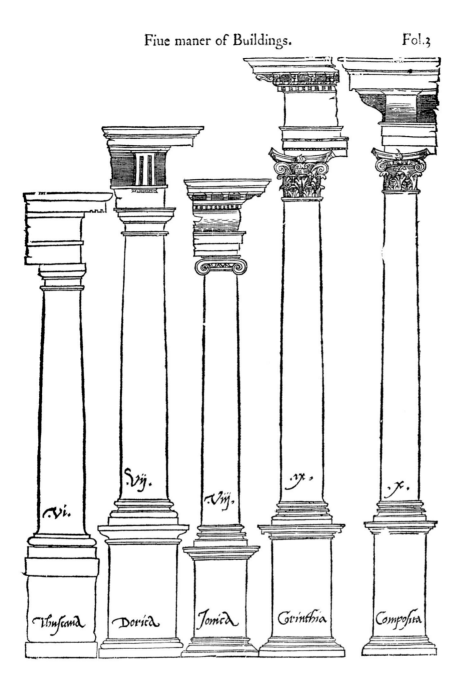

Fiue maner of Buildings.   Fol.3

Thufcana   Dorica   Jonica   Corinthia   Compofita

Fig 1.15 Comparison of the Tuscan, Doric, Ionic, Corinthian, and Composite orders, from Sebastiano Serlio, The Five Books of Architecture *(English edition of 1584; by courtesy of Dover Publications, Inc.)*

Heavily permeated by Greek thinking, the Romans continued to employ the basic principles of Greek and Hellenistic architecture, borrowing designs, products (such as statues, many of which are preserved only in Roman copies), and craftsmen. The Romans had different motives and expectations, to be sure. The first Greek revival was during the reign of Augustus (27 BCE – 14 CE), who supposedly wanted to transform Rome from a city of clay brick to one of marble. Architecture certainly took on a political agenda, and it is not surprising that buildings accumulated the richness of decoration seen, for example, in the Maison Carrée (see Fig 1.3 on page 22).

What we think of as typically Roman derives from the Imperial period, which saw many builder emperors, among them Augustus, Claudius, Vespasian, Trajan, Hadrian, and Septimius Severus. The grand scale, variety, and abundance of Roman building are predicated on the extensive use of concrete and the arch. "As concrete freed form from the constraints imposed by traditional materials, it also freed the decorative imagination from the constraints of traditional logic" (Christopher Tadgell, *Imperial Space*, p. 69). In discussing classical styles one has to realize that even in the principles (the "idiom") there was variation and evolution, as the earlier quotation from Thoreau implies.

IDENTIFYING STYLES: PRINCIPLES OF DESIGN

A carver who wishes to work skillfully in classical styles must know various aspects of design and historical precedent, as well as traditional tools and techniques. Taking the last first, tools and techniques have not changed essentially for hundreds of years, though there have been innovations in woodworking. The introduction of mahogany and other "exotics", the invention of the circular saw and the steam engine, the ability to produce raw materials such as veneers economically, might be cited as factors which influenced or engendered new styles. One could mention rotary cutters, chainsaws, and even airbrushes as having influenced contemporary styles of woodcarving. Yet the Italian cassone of the sixteenth century was carved pretty much the way we would carve it today (see Chapter 7). The pronounced difference would be in the actual construction of it, using laser-guided saw, biscuit joinery or pneumatic nailer, epoxy glue, perhaps, and synthetic finish.

The best way to learn about historic styles is to study the many reprinted Renaissance treatises and the pattern books of the eighteenth and nineteenth centuries. Also, there have been some interesting studies done in the last decade. See the Select Bibliography on pages 168–9 for these sources. It is also imperative to observe actively the historic architecture which can be found in almost any town of size, in the many historic buildings open to the public, government buildings, and city museums which have exhibitions of the decorative arts. In order to observe critically one must analyze the various aspects of each element. A style can be identified through its subject matter, composition, and treatment.

SUBJECT MATTER

An immediate indication of style may be the subject matter depicted on an architectural element or a piece of furniture. This is not an uncomplicated approach, as many motifs have been reused at different times and modified in the process. For example, the anthemion of distinctively Greek derivation, as can be seen on the necking of the column pictured in Fig 1.9 (page 25), reappears as a nearly Art Deco motif in Fig 1.16.

Almost by definition, a style includes some subjects while excluding others. The use of the leaves and fruit of the oak, laurel, olive, and grape makes sense in a classical context, while the use of goldenrod, Virginia creeper, or parsnip (as portrayed on the Bepler mantelpiece described on pages 42–3) does not. These plants were not indigenous to the Mediterranean area, had no religious or cultural significance, or were not felt to lend themselves to decoration or stylistic expression. For whatever reason, they were not assimilated into the classical design vocabulary. This is not to say that new motifs cannot be introduced into the idiom. The American architect Benjamin Latrobe (1764–1820) promoted the idea of using native plants as design motifs, and the US Capitol does indeed have capitals depicting corn (maize) and tobacco. One of the beauties of classicism is its elasticity in accommodating a range of variation.

COMPOSITION

The way the subject matter is presented—the composition—is as important to determining style as the other factors. In classicism the design is composed of as many aspects as necessary, but each of these should in some way contribute to the whole. The composition should be unified in such a way that the deletion of any aspect

Fig 1.16 An Art Deco treatment of the classical anthemion motif

would make the visual experience less satisfactory. "Thus the classical artist does not bring the form to an object from without or above, but brings it forth from within the object itself" (L'Orange, p. 9). Many carving books, such as Hasluck's *Manual of Traditional Wood Carving*, and art theory books, such as Ruskin's *Elements of Drawing*, discuss the aspects or "principles" of composition. Though terminology may differ, the list includes: order, distribution, repetition and alternation, proportion, and harmony.

Order

Order in composition denotes the underlying logic, the skeleton on which the subject matter is hung. Order includes the principles of symmetry and radiation. Classical, particularly Greek, architecture "gives the clearest possible expression of the object's particular function" (L'Orange, p. 9), and ornamentation is thoroughly integrated with the structure, often emphasizing it, as flutes emphasize the shape of a column. In contrast, seventeenth-century baroque architecture is concerned with illusionary spaces where curved walls and applied ornament tend to mask or confuse the immediate perception of structure.

Symmetry is usually thought of as a strict mirror image, but the concept can be broadened to mean "balance" in general, which allows for more variation within certain visual limits. Strict symmetry is static, while balance can be more dynamic. The apricot design presented in Chapter 2 (pages 42–52) has balance without symmetry. Rococo designs seem at first to be wildly asymmetrical, but usually are not out of balance. *Radiation* refers to the progression of elements from a central point like spokes of a wheel, or the orderly expansion from a central "backbone". The branching of a tree whose few large limbs become numerous twigs is a good example.

Distribution

Distribution is the placement of elements within the overall order of the design. In evaluating the distribution or placement of ornament there are two considerations: how the ornament embellishes the structure, and how the elements of the design relate to one another. For example, rarely, if ever, in the classical idiom do acanthus leaves or vines reach out of the prescribed "frame". Decoration can be made to give lightness or weight to a structure, depending upon its abundance, placement, and treatment.

The distribution of motifs within a design may be determined by symmetry or proportion. Certainly "weight", visual appeal, and appropriateness are factors as well. The Roman acanthus scroll appears sometimes to be as thick as a jungle, while the openness of late eighteenth-century Adam-style scrolls makes them seem lighter and less intimidating. Obviously, the object upon which the ornament is placed determines its distribution: a frieze or frieze band invites interconnected motifs (see Fig 2.8 on page 36), while a capital is more likely to be decorated with supportive or vertically oriented ornament (see Fig 1.9 on page 25 and Fig 2.5 on page 36).

Repetition and alternation

These terms refer to the use of identical elements, single or repeated, in close proximity to each other. Both egg-and-art moulding and anthemion, for instance, rely on these principles. Though repetition can give a sense of movement, "the more unmeaning an element the more it will bear repetition" (Hasluck, p. 55); conversely, the more meaning or visual interest is intended, the more demeaning repetition will be. Alternation of motifs alleviates this problem somewhat. For example, the close spacing of the eggs on Greek moulding is abandoned in eighteenth-century examples, which often stretch the "baskets"

Fig 1.17 Egg-and-dart moulding (top) with enlarged egg "baskets", from the Lenygon Collection (Colonial Williamsburg Foundation/ Frederick Wilbur)

Fig 1.18 Variant egg-and-dart moulding with shells substituted for eggs, from the Lenygon Collection (Colonial Williamsburg Foundation/Frederick Wilbur)

containing the eggs (Fig 1.17), and literally depict flared darts between them, thus making each element or unit more perceptible. They may also add variety by including other motifs, such as shells and flowers (Fig 1.18).

Contrast or variety may be seen as corollaries to repetition and alternation. Examples of contrast include the combination of angular shapes with curvilinear ones; the use of projecting shapes in opposition to recessed ones; and the use of surface textures which reflect light differently (see the apricot sequence on pages 42–52.)

Proportion

One way to vary a composition is to emphasize one element over another—to change its proportions. *Size* is a simple measurement, and *scale* is the size of something in relation to another object, but *proportion* is the relationship between similar elements. Strictly, a proportion is an equality between two ratios. As one understands the classical orders, it becomes clear that although two Ionic temples, for instance, are of different overall sizes, the relationship of column height to overall height remains the same, or the width of the frieze has the same relationship to the height of the column. All components bear a uniform relationship to all the other components, regardless of the overall size of the structure.

When we say something is "out of proportion", we are comparing what is seen to a visualized situation where at least one object is different. For example, a huge vase sitting on a small table appears too big—dominating, disguising, or destabilizing the arrangement. We visualize a larger table surface which would put the vase in a more harmonious relationship, reveal its relationship with the supporting surface, and make it less vulnerable to tipping over. (Or vice versa: we visualize a smaller vase on the original table.) Though the reader may disagree, to my eye the canopied overmantel by Emma Bepler illustrated

in Chapter 2 (pages 42–3) is ponderously top-heavy. The columns with their cushion capitals appear massive enough by themselves, but the outline, structure, and profuse decoration of the overmantel overpower these columns. I dare say that even the original context of the piece could not have countered this feeling. I think also that the oak-leaf carvings, though wonderfully realistic, are incompatible with, and out of proportion to, the fine, lacy, incised carvings of the panels above.

Harmony

Harmony implies unity, and the execution of all the elements of a composition in a congenial manner; "An intended unity must be the result of composition," states Ruskin (*Elements of Drawing*, p. 162). A composition is a selection of various objects, manmade or natural, whose arrangement has been artificially manipulated. Though a piece of driftwood or a stone may be intriguing or visually interesting, they are not art by themselves. Each aspect of composition must work organically with the others to produce a successful, harmonious design.

TREATMENT

The third aspect in analyzing style is treatment. Treatment is the actual presentation of the subject matter and the composition of it. It is not misleading to say that treatment and technique are nearly the same; surely technique produces treatment. Treatments may differ in their use of detail, relief, surface texture, or finish. One should consider the degree to which a representation depicts naturalistic details, or is reduced to essential, abstract, forms. Often the sheer amount of detail is the most characteristic feature of a particular treatment. The depth or superficiality of relief (discussed more fully in Chapter 2) may reflect a particular style: compare the Art Deco relief of Fig 2.41 (page 46) with the figures of Or San Michele in Fig 2.51 (page 50).

What we usually think of as "technique" is synonymous with the use of tools to create the physical subject matter of a composition. Various tools can be used to fabricate the forms, create relief, and define details. A carving may have a rough or a smooth surface, crisp or ragged arrises, regular depth of ground, or an appropriate level of detail, all of which contribute to the quality of execution. In replicating classical motifs in wood, the architectural carver should understand traditional techniques in order to achieve a viable rendition. In succeeding chapters, the possibilities of treatment will be discussed and demonstrated. It is worth studying the photographic examples for subject matter and composition as well as technique.

RELIEF CARVING

Types of relief • Working methods

Relief carving and sculpture are the two main categories of woodcarving. Sculpture, or carving in the round, is generally freestanding and is intended to offer a viable representation from multiple points of view. Human figures, animals, and abstract forms are common subjects. In relief carving, the shape or form represented is associated with a background or structural context. The background may be flat, curved, obscured, or even just implied. It may be textured, diapered, or represent a landscape. Most architectural carving can be considered as some variety of relief carving, whether it is a repeating leaf along a profiled moulding, a volute on the side of a scrolled bracket, or a bird "flying" across a mountainous landscape. The techniques used to express the design can range from a "drawing" consisting of incised lines to a "sculptural" high relief. Though three-dimensional sculpture is often integrated with an architectural context, it generally does not become a part of the structure in the way that decorative or relief ornament does, though admittedly the distinction can become one of semantics. The caryatids of the Erechtheion in Athens—full-length female figures standing in for columns—are a famous exception. On the other hand, relief carving is not confined to the structural elements of furniture or buildings, but can be used self-sufficiently in a plaque, sign, coat of arms, or similar application.

In this chapter the conventional idea of forms projecting from a background will be explored. The notion of relief carving is so fundamental to decorative carving that it will reappear in all succeeding chapters. As with other pictorial media, such as painting or mosaic, there are problems involved in the portrayal of natural or even geometric objects. Though some paintings look so real that they might be the scene outside one's window, they rely completely on illusion to achieve this effect. With woodcarving there is at least some small reality of depth; even woodblock prints and incised designs are created by the removal of wood. As we will see, there is a spectrum of reality, depending on the amount of relief in the carved objects. Yet some things—spider webs, flames, smoke, or sunbeams—are either too diaphanous or intangible to be literally portrayed, or are beyond the scope of the material. Such things can be depicted through convention, suggestion, or even illusion, however.

> *Get the masses in proper perspective, so that a good balance exists between all parts, . . . and the design will be a success.*
>
> FRED T. HODGSON,
> *PRACTICAL WOODCARVING*

Any given piece of wood is essentially monochromatic, having a limited range of color. Yes, there are striped patterns, wonderful reds and yellows, and exquisitely figured grain, but woods when carved are generally without differentiating colors. The grain of the wood may, in fact, be detrimental to the clarity of the relief. The effectiveness of the relief is dependent on the relative differences in reflected light or in strength of shadow. Shadow is produced by the differing projection of elements, and the varying angles of surfaces. In Fig 2.1 the hemisphere, low-angled pyramid, and square projection illustrate how shadow defines shape: the right sides of the forms are easily perceived, while the left sides tend to blend with the background. Notice that the hemisphere with its sloping sides seems the most readable of the three. The vertical left wall of the square is completely lost. The varied reflections of light on the different planes of the pyramid are more important to perception than shadow as such.

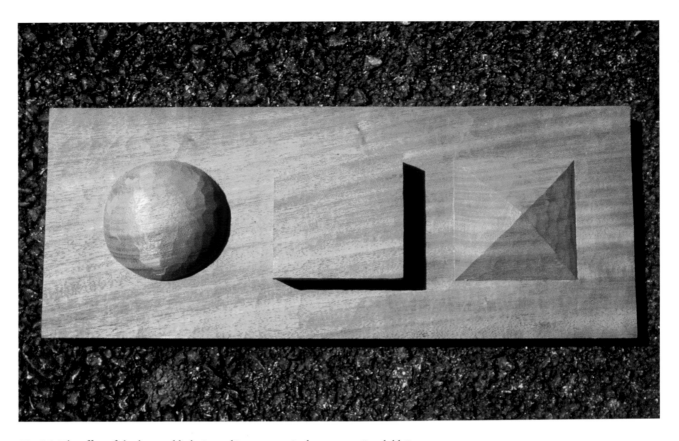

Fig 2.1 The effect of shadow and light in making geometric shapes more "readable"

Shadow can be produced by texture as well as by relief. In Fig 2.38 (page 45) the stippling creates numerous shadows which contrast with the flat surface design. Though an element may be painted completely white, shadow still allows the form to be seen. By comparing the series of apricot panels featured later in this chapter (pages 42–52) one can readily see the differing readability of the various types of relief.

In many carved objects, and particularly in landscape scenes, there is a requirement to make the portrayal convincing—to give it what in fiction is called "verisimilitude". There are several ways to achieve this believability. As in two-dimensional painting, the laws of perspective can be used. Perspective is the principle that objects further from the eye appear smaller than those which are closer. Usually in decorative carving the various elements contained in front of the background are not separated by much distance, and thus do not require this consideration. At times, however, making the primary element (the part with most projection) slightly larger than those nearer to the background helps to accentuate their different positions, creating an enhanced illusion of depth. "In a broad sense, any visual perception which does not harmonize with physical measurements may be termed an 'illusion'" (M. Luckiesh, *Visual Illusions*, p. 10). In a sense, therefore, woodcarvers can be thought of as illusionists or magicians.

Though relief carving implies form, perceiving solid form is a more complex operation and one prone to more confusion than perceiving and understanding outline. One can draw something which doesn't translate into a readily carvable object. Consequently, carved designs generally should have strong outlines. Line by itself can evoke an aesthetic or emotional response. Straight lines are not as provocative as curved ones; angular lines are more "energetic" than calmly curving ones. Verticality implies strength and aspiration, while the horizontal conveys repose and quiet. We all develop certain ways of seeing, based on experience and convention, and anomalies such as leaves twisted so as to look like propellers, or a pyramid balanced on its apex, would not "read" well. A good example is the fact that a face in profile is more easily perceived in relief than one shown frontally: thus portraits on coins or memorial plaques are usually in profile. Relief carving does permit the overlap of elements such as leaves, vines, arms, and legs. Even on simple foliage mouldings, secondary leaves peek out from between the primary leaves to fill the ground.

THE ARCHITECTURAL CONTEXT

In classical architecture there are several areas which lend themselves to relief decoration. In addition to the well-known capitals, Greek and Roman temples were often decorated with carving in the **tympanum** of the pediment and on the frieze of the entablature. Of course, many mouldings associated with these components were also embellished.

The Doric frieze, famously epitomized in the Parthenon, is divided into **metopes** and **triglyphs**. The metopes frequently contain relief carvings: of warriors fighting centaurs and Amazons, or perhaps symbols such as trophies (groups of weapons and armor), bucrania (bulls' heads), torches or lamps, and items symbolic of professions or personages (Figs 2.2 and 2.3).

The frieze of the Ionic and Corinthian orders is not interrupted by triglyphs and often contains a continuous design. The procession of Civil War soldiers marching around the Pension Bureau building in Washington, DC (Fig 2.4) is a good example. Other examples are continuously repeating motifs such as the acanthus scrolls on the Maison Carrée at Nîmes, France (Fig 2.5) and the Palazzo Bevilacqua at Verona, Italy (Fig 2.6). Sometimes isolated motifs are repeated, such as the griffins guarding a torch on the temple of Antoninus and Faustina in the Forum at Rome (Fig 2.7).

Frieze band is a general term denoting any horizontal band which is decorated in the same way as a frieze. In addition to those ornaments previously mentioned, floral garlands and drapery swags often connect bucrania,

Fig 2.2 Trophy panels and bucrania of Doric frieze, Piazza Bra, Verona, Italy

Fig 2.3 A bucranium panel suitable for a Doric frieze

Fig 2.4 The glazed terracotta frieze of the Pension Bureau in Washington, DC (now the National Building Museum), built in 1887 to serve Civil War pensioners

Fig 2.5 *The acanthus scroll (or rinceau) on the Corinthian frieze of the Maison Carrée, Nîmes (by courtesy of the Musée Archéologique, Nîmes, France)*

Fig 2.8 *Ionic frieze at the University of Virginia, Charlottesville, VA, consisting of garlands, cherubs, and bucrania*

Fig 2.6 *Acanthus scroll on the Palazzo Bevilacqua, Verona, Italy*

Fig 2.9 *Cherubs and garlands in the frieze of Or San Michele, Florence, Italy*

Fig 2.7 *Griffins on the frieze of the temple of Antoninus and Faustina, in the Forum, Rome*

cherubs, torches, and other ornaments (Figs 2.8 and 2.9). The floral garland of Fig 2.10, however, is a self-contained panel, as is the drapery swag of Fig 2.11. The laurel swag connects ram's heads on a lamp-post base in Fig 2.12, and a circular wreath is often used on memorials (Fig 2.13; see also Fig 6.26 on page 129). In many instances this band is decorated with plant motifs, such as the characteristically

Fig 2.10 *Cherubs holding floral garland, in a frieze at St Paul's Cathedral, London*

Fig 2.11 *Drapery swag, London*

Fig 2.12 *Laurel-leaf swags suspended between rams' heads on base of lamp-post, Lexington, VA*

Fig 2.13 *Laurel wreath on the base of a statue of Andrea Palladio, Vicenza, Italy. A plumb level is included to symbolize the architect's profession*

Greek anthemion (Fig 2.14; see also Fig 6.3 on page 120) or the acanthus scroll (see Figs 2.6 and 2.74, pages 36 and 59); or with animals, as in Fig 2.15 with its alternating dolphins and urns of flowers.

For the most part, the tympana of temple pediments contained sculptures of gods and heroes, as on the Parthenon at Athens (the so-called Elgin marbles, now at the British Museum in London). In time, however, many motifs came to be used to fill the space. Cartouches (discussed in Chapter 3), urns with fruit or flowers (Fig 2.16),

Fig 2.14 *Anthemion frieze, Cincinnati, OH. The "Greek key" fret is another example of a running design*

Fig 2.15 *Frieze of dolphins and floral vases, Florence, Italy*

Fig 2.16 *Relief carving of urn in pediment, Court House, Staunton, VA. The scrolling acanthus terminates in rams' heads*

or symbols of one kind or another are found here, at times filling the triangular space, at other times simply centered within it. Segmental pediments also can be filled with ornament, as in Fig 2.17.

Relief **panels**, which may be used in a number of architectural contexts, are contained in a defined geometric space. As noted above, the square metope of the Doric frieze often contains rosettes, figures, or symbols. There are dozens of possible symbols (see the books by Biedermann, Hall, and Lewis & Darley listed in the Select Bibliography). Fig 2.18 shows a square door panel with a high-relief eagle holding a shield of Rome. The panel in

the Vatican (Fig 2.19) depicts what is termed **grotesque** ornament: in this case two **addorsed** or back-to-back half-figures with foliage swirling around them. Derived from ancient Roman wall paintings, the term *grotesque* denotes loosely composed foliage associated with human and mythological figures as well as exotic animals and birds. It tends to be symmetrically arranged and treated with a fanciful lightness. Two additional examples are shown in Fig 2.20.

Rectangular panels are probably the most common, because this is the shape defined by the structural rails and stiles of a door or a piece of case furniture. Fig 2.21 shows one of a group of floral panels on a door in Vicenza, Italy. The grouping of objects on the side door of the Duomo Santa Maria del Fiore, Florence (Figs 2.22 and 2.23), is isolated and unique. The panel from the Vatican in Fig 2.24 is framed by egg-and-dart moulding in the manner of a tablet (to be discussed in Chapter 3). The arrangement of two animals face to face (**affronted**) with urn or torch between them is a common antique as well as Renaissance motif (see Figs 2.7 and 2.74, pages 36 and 59).

A shape quite often seen in the Renaissance is the space defined by the outline of a square superimposed on a circle, or a lozenge shape with semicircles attached to each side, reflecting the intense interest in geometry

Fig 2.17 Shield carving in a segmental pediment, Chelsea, London. Note the garland relief panel above, and the fans in the spandrels of the fanlight

Fig 2.18 Door panel of eagle holding shield, Rome

Fig 2.19 Shutter panel in the Vatican Museums, Rome (photograph by F. Wilbur used by permission of the Vatican Museums)

Fig 2.20 (Right and below right) *Grotesque designs from Italian Renaissance sources, the lower one from Santa Maria dei Miracoli, Venice, Italy (by permission of Dover Publications, Inc.)*

Fig 2.21 (Below) *Low-relief carving on door panel, framed by bolection moulding, Casa Pigafetta, Vicenza, Italy*

at this period. The bronze door panels by Lorenzo Ghiberti (1378–1455) at St John's Baptistery in Florence are fine examples.

Long vertical panels on **pilasters**, doorjambs, picture frames, and mantel uprights are often carved with interlacing vines and **candelabra** forms (Fig 2.25). Though there are several varieties, the candelabra device is made up of a central "turning" of urn or vase shapes which provides a support for swirling foliage, festoons, birds, fanciful creatures, and so forth. (See Chapter 7 for further examples of the candelabra motif.) The grotesque panels in Fig 2.20 also have a central candelabra form.

Tondi (**tondo**, singular) or **roundels** are circular panels containing a variety of ornamentation, from floral groups to animals, symbolic objects, and trophies. The arch of Constantine has eight figural tondi (Fig 2.26). The **medallion** is an oval or circular panel, usually containing a portrait as in Fig 2.27. An odd shape, but one frequently decorated, is the **spandrel** of an arch, as shown in Fig 2.28. There are, of course, other panel shapes to accommodate a specific location.

Fig 2.22 *Relief carving on Duomo Santa Maria del Fiore, Florence, Italy (photograph by courtesy of Kevin Maxson)*

Fig 2.24 *Door panel in the Vatican Museums (photograph by F. Wilbur, used by permission of the Vatican Museums)*

Fig 2.25 *Pilaster panel, Piazza dei Signori, Verona, Italy*

Fig 2.23 *A detail of the carving in Fig 2.22 (photograph by courtesy of Kevin Maxson)*

Fig 2.26 Tondo on the Arch of Constantine, Rome (312 CE)

Fig 2.27 Medallion on the door of the Duomo S. Maria del Fiore, Florence (by courtesy of Kevin Maxson)

Fig 2.28 Spandrel carving on the Arch of Septimius Severus, the Forum, Rome

TYPES OF RELIEF

Most instruction books on woodcarving explain the process of relief carving, but fail to explore the entire range of possibilities, the ways in which they may be combined, or their appropriate uses. The following descriptions center on a series of carvings which show the same design carved in a range of different techniques. I have designed a twig of apricots and leaves in an uncomplicated form, without overlapping elements, in order to illustrate the simpler techniques and the effects of shadow, line, and relief.

The apricot most familiar to the grocery shopper is *Prunus armeniaca*, the Mediterranean or California apricot. Seen in monochrome, the fruits look similar to plums or even peaches. The leaves are somewhat heart-shaped with serrations visible near the pointed end, and the center vein (actually on the back of the leaf) is exaggerated in the carving to emphasize the flow of the design. The round shape of the fruit (technically a *drupe*) and the flattish planes of the leaves present an attractive contrast of form. Fig 2.29 shows the basic design, and the contrasting treatments are illustrated on pages 43–52.

Compare these samples with the mantelpiece in Fig 2.30. This is decidedly not an example of classical restraint: most surfaces are covered with a variety of carving techniques, and stylized plants are interspersed with naturalistic ones. There are no references to classical mouldings, capitals, or pediment structure. Even wild parsnip leaves stand in for the classical acanthus. It is, however, a wonderful example of the various types of relief discussed below; it is a veritable sampler of carving techniques. It was carved in 1893–4 by Emma Bepler during the flowering of the Cincinnati (Ohio) decorative arts, a movement which concentrated mainly on art-carved furniture and art pottery. It reflects the tenets of the Aesthetic Movement, which most reference books summarize as one of "art for art's sake". Derived from a variety of sources, including the writings of Ruskin and Eastlake and the motifs of Asian art, the Aesthetic Movement considered art as a life philosophy and propounded that the decorative arts, by virtue of being handcrafted and inspired by the natural world, could be morally elevating. "The artist had a moral obligation to raise the quality of life of the viewer (or the user)" (Jennifer Howe, *Cincinnati Art-Carved Furniture and Interiors*, p. 66).

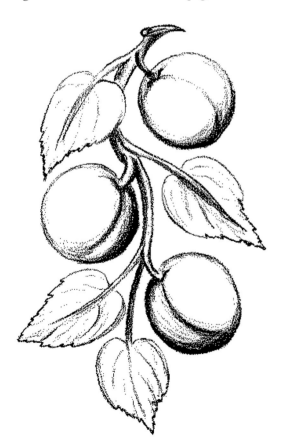 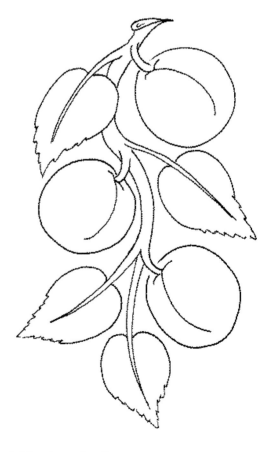

Fig 2.29 Drawings of the apricot panel used for the following examples: shaded drawing and outline cartoon

Fig 2.30 *Mantelpiece carved by Emma Bepler, 1893–4 (gift of Mrs Carl W. Bieser; photograph by courtesy of the Cincinnati Art Museum, Cincinnati, OH)*

Fig 2.31 *Incised carving*

The Bepler piece and many others are on view as part of the permanent Cincinnati Wing exhibit at the Cincinnati Art Museum; to my knowledge, the finest group of late nineteenth-century art-carved furniture in the USA.

INCISED CARVING

Incised designs are those which are carved into the surface of the material and have no relief; but the technique is included here because it is sometimes used in conjunction with relief techniques. (See, for example, the back wings of the griffins in Fig 2.73, page 59.) Simple V-grooves made with a parting tool are most like a two-dimensional line drawing. The parting tool is so called because the design is "parted" from the surrounding surface. The panel in Fig 2.31 depicts the outlines of the apricots and leaves, but there is no modeling. The top leaf, which overlaps the twig, is slightly larger, to emphasize that it is more "forward" than the others. The graphic

Fig 2.32 *Detail of the Bepler mantelpiece showing incised asters and goldenrod, flat carving along vertical elements, and below-surface carving of rosettes (gift of Mrs Carl W. Bieser; photograph by courtesy of the Cincinnati Art Museum, Cincinnati, OH)*

depiction of wild asters and goldenrod in Fig 2.32 has some shallow modeling within the outline, but the form is still at the surface.

Incised lettering, typical of Greek and Roman monuments, is similar, but is a specialized field (see Chapter 3). Incised lines can be found in other varieties of relief to depict shallow lines such as veins of leaves or spider webs, or texturing, as on the caps of acorns. Chip carving is also classed as incised carving, though it is a highly specialized technique.

"FLAT" CARVING

Older carving manuals use this term to describe a design remaining essentially two-dimensional and at the surface, but with a recessed background (Fig 2.33). This technique is a good vehicle to practice setting-in by matching the tool sweeps to the curves of the design. One should excavate the ground only slightly. For this 6 × 9in (152 × 229mm) panel the ground is ⅛in (3mm) deep. This technique also gives good practice in grounding evenly to the same depth. To check the depth, sight at an angle to compare the side walls. Though fishtail grounders

Fig 2.34 Using the frontbent shallow gouge for grounding in tight spots

(#2 or #3 in the Pfeil numbering, sweep 3 or 4 Sheffield List numbering) are very helpful, a narrow frontbent grounder (Pfeil #3 or equivalent) is indispensable for grounding evenly in tight areas (Fig 2.34). The fruit in Fig 2.33 has been lightly modeled; to represent it by a plain circle would look quite ridiculous. This illustrates that design and technique go hand in hand—some representations work better than others.

Flat carving is not necessarily "crude", though it is uncomplicated. Its bold effect may be entirely appropriate to a context such as the Art Deco panels of Fig 2.35. The picture frame with oak leaves in Figs 2.36 and 2.37 works a little better than the apricot sample, though here again the acorns are rounded slightly; note also the incised lines on the cap. The round coaster or trivet of Fig 2.38 has no modeling at all, except where the tongue lolls from the mouth. The leaves on the vertical elements in Fig 2.32 are flat to the profiled surface, with minimal relief to indicate overlapping and a few incised lines to represent veins.

Included in this category are **strapwork** designs, which consist of bands that overlap one another, sometimes combined with scrolls or other attached ornament.

Fig 2.33 "Flat" carving with only slight modeling

Fig 2.35 Art Deco panels, Richmond, VA

They are not as "tight" as Celtic knotwork designs, nor do they resemble the running designs known as frets. Strapwork was a common motif in later Renaissance England, particularly in the Jacobean period (1603–25).

To make the flat surfaces stand out, this sort of carving is often stippled, punched, or "padded". One woodcarving myth is that punching is to be avoided, as it is often used to cover poor grounding. This may sometimes be true, but punching is a useful technique to make the outlines more visible by way of contrast. A nail can be used for bold work, but this is quite tedious, as you can imagine. A punch with many points can be made from a soft metal bar stock or rod by filing with a triangular mill file. First make a series of parallel valleys, and then a second series perpendicular to the first, creating a regular field of pyramids. One can purchase this style of punch in different sizes. Some supply houses also have stamps with designs such as stars, acorns, and flowers. These can be used to create a diaper-like background. (There is more about diaper patterns in Chapter 7.)

Fig 2.36 Picture frame using the "flat" carving technique. (The watercolor Legacy *by Mark A. Collins is included by permission)*

Fig 2.38 Trivet, showing how stippling adds to the readability of the "flat" carving

Fig 2.37 A detail of the frame in Fig 2.36

BELOW-SURFACE CARVING

This technique is cousin to incised carving, but interior areas are fully modeled (Fig 2.39). The object depicted does not project beyond the surrounding surface; the ground usually slopes from the original surface to "behind" the object depicted. The ground may slope inward, or it may be implied or barely visible, as in the rosettes of Fig 2.32. Below-surface carving is also termed **coelanaglyphic relief**, *intaglio rilevato*, *cavo-rilievo*, or "sunken" relief. The door panel in Fig 2.40 is a good example, as is the panel in Fig 2.41. This term may also be used for the ancient Egyptian method of relief in which the object is outlined with incised lines and then modeled. The surrounding surface is not part of the decoration but forms a frame around the relief, and there is no recessed background.

Fig 2.40 *Below-surface carving on a door panel, Florence, Italy*

Fig 2.39 *Below-surface carving*

Fig 2.41 *Below-surface carving, Cincinnati Bell Building, Cincinnati, OH*

INTAGLIO

Though the dictionary defines *intaglio* with words such as "incised" or "engraved", carvers often use the term in a more specific way. In a sense it is the opposite of relief, because the areas of the design with the most projection are the most deeply carved. This sort of carving is used as a negative pattern to impress a soft material or to mold plaster or composition, or generally to transfer an image to another material. The Scandinavian butter mold in Fig 2.42 opens to reveal a hunk of butter with designs raised

from the surface. Signet rings and seals leave a projecting image in the wax, as does the die used to stamp coins. Fig 2.43 shows the apricot design with a plaster cast made directly from the intaglio carving. As you can see, the carving has to be exactly opposite to the desired result. Remember that in order for the intaglio to be used as a mold, there can be no undercutting, but the design must have "draft". This means that all walls should have at least a few degrees of outward slope so that the material can be extricated without breakage.

Fig 2.42 Intaglio carving in a butter mold

Fig 2.43 Intaglio carving, with the casting made directly from it

BASSO-RILIEVO

This Italian term has long been used to denote low-relief sculpture (*bas-relief* in French) in which the furthest projection of the portrayed objects is less than one half of the real-life depth. The apricots in Fig 2.44 are only ¼in (6mm) in relief, though they represent fruit with a 1½ or 2in (38–50mm) diameter. Coins are excellent examples of the illusion of depth in extremely shallow relief. Fig 2.45 shows a cast-iron lamp-post at the Philadelphia Museum of Art. This technique may be appropriate for furniture and other items subject to wear and tear, for smaller items and those which will be viewed closely. Fig 2.46 shows a variation of our simple apricot motif, in which more elements overlap. This design still retains the flow of the simpler version, but has a more three-dimensional, naturalistic, and less graphic feel, even though it remains contained within its frame or border.

Fig 2.45 Basso-rilievo *on a cast metal lamp-post at the Philadelphia Museum of Art*

Fig 2.44 Basso-rilievo

Fig 2.46 A basso-rilievo *variation on the apricot design, showing more overlap between the elements*

MEZZO-RILIEVO

Medium relief is where half the natural thickness of the object is carved (Fig 2.47). According to art historian John Canaday, "Mezzo rilievo probably offers the happiest combination of absolute integration with architecture along with sufficient freedom for independent creative expression on the part of the sculptor" (*What is Art?*, p. 39). Curiously, in order to produce the appearance of relief one actually carves away the background. As the relief brings the leaves of the apricot panel away from the background, the two upper leaves turn more edgewise to the viewer, creating a more in-the-round character. This makes for a nice contrast with the rounded fruits. The figures on a fragment in the Roman Forum (Fig 2.48) and in the spandrels on the arch of Septimius Severus (see Fig 2.28, page 41) are in *mezzo-rilievo*.

ALTO-RILIEVO

High relief depicts approximately three-quarters or more of the object's thickness (Fig 2.49). This implies a high degree of undercutting to bring the forms away from

Fig 2.48 Fragment with figures in mezzo-rilievo, *in the Forum, Rome*

Fig 2.47 Mezzo-rilievo

Fig 2.49 Alto-rilievo

the ground. (Another technique to achieve this effect is applied carving, discussed below.) The grape leaves on the door of the Duomo Santa Maria del Fiore are life-sized (Fig 2.50), while the sculptors of Or San Michele appear to be free of the background, and could almost walk around their shop (Fig 2.51). The detail of the oak leaf on the Emma Bepler mantelpiece is a nice example as well (Fig 2.52).

These distinctions may sound somewhat academic, but they are helpful in communicating a general understanding of the depth of the carving. Of course, several varieties of relief can and often do appear on the same carving, especially when a number of objects are grouped together. Several visual adjustments can be used to imply more depth. Size differences between elements, placement of various elements, and perspective or implied relative positions all help to portray depth. The rhythmic cadence of the marching soldiers on the Pension Building frieze (see Fig 2.4, page 35) creates an almost rippling effect. Contrasting the *mezzo-rilievo* of the first rank of soldiers with the *basso-rilievo* of the second rank also creates depth, but note that the rifle barrels are all on the

Fig 2.52 Oak-leaf carving in alto-rilievo *on the Bepler mantelpiece (gift of Mrs Carl W. Bieser; photograph by courtesy of the Cincinnati Art Museum, Cincinnati, OH)*

same plane. The appropriateness of one type of relief over another may depend on distance to viewer, lighting, vulnerability to wear, or the emotional effect desired.

On some of the apricot panels, the surrounding "frame" has been lowered to allow the twig and leaves to overlap it. The ground of each has been recessed a small amount below these elements. As one can appreciate, the deep recesses of *alto-relievo* require lots of time and careful manipulation of tools, and having a frame at the level of the original surface adds undue difficulty. More often than not, the relief panel is grounded all the way to the edge and held in a separate frame made of rails and stiles. The grapevine panel of Santa Maria del Fiore (see Fig 2.50) is a clear illustration. Sometimes a **bolection** moulding is used to hold the panel in place. This overlaps the rails and stiles, as well as the panel (see Fig 2.21, page 39). Standing proud of the frame, the bolection has more framing "presence" than an ordinary panel moulding (as in Fig 2.19, page 38), which lies inside the rails and stiles.

The deep voids of *alto-rilievo* can be wasted by "drilling" with a semicircular gouge. After lightly defining the circle, hold the handle of the gouge between palms and spin the tool. A similar technique was used extensively by

Fig 2.50 Alto-rilievo *carving on one of the doors of the Duomo, Florence*

Fig 2.51 Alto-rilievo *scene of sculptors at work, Or San Michele, Florence*

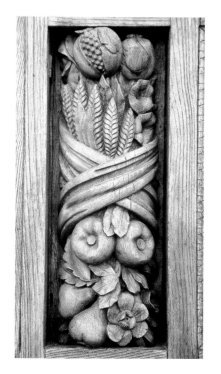

Fig 2.53 Applied carving of vegetables on the door of Santa Croce, Florence

Roman sculptors in stone, and the effect is sometimes very obvious. Frontbent gouges are also helpful in working the severe undercutting which is often necessary.

We noted above that stippling the background of shallow relief adds contrast and readability, but in higher-relief carving it is quite unnecessary because the forms create shadow; compare Fig 2.49 with Fig 2.38.

APPLIED CARVING

In applied carvings the design is cut out, often pierced, then carved separately from the ground, and finally fastened to another board which becomes the ground. Ultimately, the result should appear the same as a relief carving, especially when placed in a framing recess. The group of vegetables in Fig 2.53 is an example of applied carving. The panel in Fig 2.54 comprises a flat background with a parted line to indicate the frame, and the separate carving (Fig 2.55) applied. This technique allows one to carve the forms nearly in the round, thus creating an *alto-rilievo*. Most of the carvings of Grinling Gibbons

Fig 2.54 Applied carving

Fig 2.55 The same applied carving before being attached to its background

are applied: they are fixed to a wall or a backing board, often in multiple layers. This method can be advantageous, as it may save material, facilitate undercutting, be more practical in its installation, or give quite a dramatic effect if carved from a wood which contrasts in color with the background.

After transferring the design and cutting it out with the bandsaw, one can secure the blank by screwing it to a backing board or work station as explained on the following pages. The oft-touted method of glue and paper is, I feel, a last resort. It is an appropriate alternative when parts are too thin, or mounting screws would foul tools. Extreme care must be taken in extricating the piece from the paper when complete.

Applied carving allows for back-cutting, which gives the effect of undercutting, but working from the back of the carving after the piece has been freed from its mounting board. Of course, all other carving and undercutting should be done before removing the carving from the backing board. Often back-cutting can be done with a knife.

PIERCED CARVING

Applied carvings are in effect pierced carvings applied to a ground. In pierced carving there is no background, as it has been cut away (Figs 2.56 and 2.57). Obviously there needs to be considerable thought as to how the elements will be supported. It is advisable to have some overlap with the frame. After cutting the negative spaces, the carving method is the same as for relief. Depending upon the location, both sides may need to be carved. In this case the carving becomes truly sculptural, and carved elements may straddle the frame.

As one can readily see by the comparative examples above, there is a fairly direct correlation between depth of relief and the possibilities for realistic depiction. The lower the relief, the more dependence there is on outline; whereas deeply modeled forms make their visual impact through the shadows they produce. The Italian cassone in Chapter 7 illustrates several of these techniques.

Fig 2.56 Pierced carving

Fig 2.57 Applied carving for mantel frieze block, Blandfield, Caret, VA (home of Mrs James C. Wheat). The photograph shows the pierced carving before application

WORKING METHODS

Design, material, and tools are the three crucial aspects of any craft. Design may derive from historical precedent or may be generated by the artisan. The carver may be asked to carve a variety of woods. In order to translate the design effectively to the material, one must know how to employ one's tools skillfully, whether chainsaws or modified gouges for specific situations.

If one is not restricted by outside parameters, design and wood species should be considered together. The material should "hold" the forms well—meaning that the intended location, depth of relief, delicacy of detail, grain properties, and finish should all be taken into account when selecting the wood. Carving thin, delicate detail in red oak (*Quercus rubra*), for instance, with its open grain and consequent weak areas, is frustrating. Also, its bold grain patterns may obscure the finer shadows. On the other hand, forms are readily perceived in bland, light-colored basswood (*Tilia americana*), but it is soft and easily marred or stained. In relief carving one is removing material from one side of the board, so some thought should be given to the stability of the species used.

It should not need saying that one should always maintain tools in good condition, keeping them sharp and stored (or laid out on the bench) in an orderly manner. The workpiece should always be properly secured. For most projects, clamping directly to the bench top is best, but fixing to a backing board or using a work station of some kind is usually as efficient. Of course, if your bench has dog holes, make use of them whenever it is appropriate and safe to do so. There are a number of specialized jigs and fixtures one can produce for specific situations, but the simple and versatile work station described below will address most ordinary needs.

A SIMPLE WORK STATION

Adapted from various fixtures described in older carving manuals, the work station shown in Fig 2.58 is an uncomplicated way to hold the carving blank and to protect the table or bench. It is easily made and extremely versatile, requiring only a 14 x 28in (355 x 710mm) piece of smooth and dense plywood (such as 5-ply birch-veneered plywood), some scraps of the same, and some small pieces of hardwood. One might want a larger size, but if the carving is very large it can probably be clamped

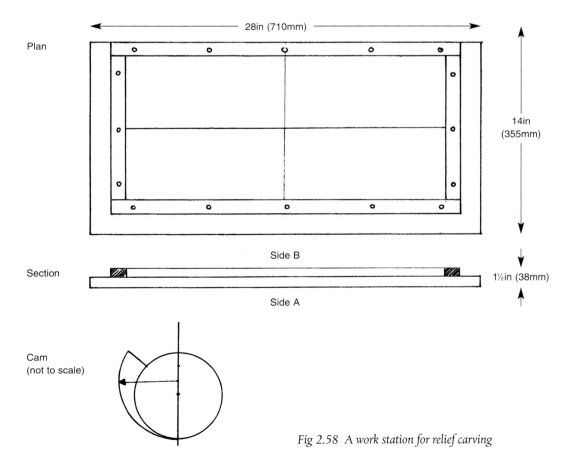

Fig 2.58 A work station for relief carving

directly to the bench or tabletop anyway. This station allows one to work at any table which is sturdy and without excessive vibration.

Both sides of the board are used. The flat side holds flat-backed blanks by screwing from the fence side into the back of the blank (Fig 2.59). The second side has fences and various filler strips which hold the work by means of a pair of wedges or cams (Fig 2.60).

After cutting the piece of plywood, mark the length and width centerlines on the side which will hold flat carvings (side A in Fig 2.58). These will come in handy for locating screws and aligning blanks. For work which has symmetrically curved silhouettes, a system of gridlines could be marked on the plywood as well. The second side (B) has four fences screwed and glued to it. On three sides they are set in from the edges by 1½in (38mm); the fourth fence is even with the remaining edge of the plywood. This is the basic unit upon which temporary fences and holding jigs are screwed. (Remember that because the "box" is offset, any gridlines drawn on this side will

be different from those on the flat side.) Make generous countersinks for the screws so they don't mar the table or bench, and so that there is little chance of chipping a carving tool on them. Round over the outside edges to prevent splinters and unnecessary wear on the hands. The end flanges allow the work station to be clamped to the bench without interference from the clamps. Newspaper or a rubber mat can be used to protect the tabletop.

To hold a rectangular blank in the work station, cut several pieces of scrap plywood to fit between the long fences, and screw them to the ground. If additional restraint is needed, scrap pieces can be used as fillers, and wedges or cams can be used to tighten the blank. Make several pairs of wedges from a hard wood. It is advisable to have them thicker than the plywood fences so that they can be coaxed loose when necessary. Several cams can be cut from the scrap plywood. They are simple spirals, laid out as in Fig 2.58. The diameter of the circle needs to be slightly less than the space available. Draw the circle and then divide the radius into thirds. Using the point nearest the center, draw an arc outwards from any point on the circumference, approximately one third of the way around the circle. It is not usually necessary to screw the cams to the board: use them loose, like wedges.

There are two possibilities for securing irregular shapes such as the bracket in Fig 2.60. One is to save the waste from the bandsawn blank and use it as a filler piece between fence and blank. It may need to be reduced in thickness so that it doesn't interfere with the carving. The second is to place the blank on a scrap piece of plywood and trace around the profile. This outline is then bandsawn, and the negative part acts as a form or filler piece.

Fig 2.59 A cartouche mounted on the "A"-side of the work station, fastened by screws through the back

Fig 2.60 A console bracket held by a bandsawn spacer and cams on the "B"-side of the work station

Because it is difficult to bandsaw the outline exactly, some fitting may be required. A thin rubber or foam strip can be placed between the blank and the form to take up the slack. Homemade cleats of various configurations, as well as commercially available toggle clamps, can be screwed to the work station to hold the edges of the blank.

The lengthwise lip at the front holds short lengths of moulding. Egg-and-dart moulding, which is worked from both top and front, is a good example. If the moulding has been mitered, angled cleats can be screwed or clamped to the work station as in Fig 2.61. Otherwise, blocks which match the moulding profile can clamp the moulding directly (Fig 2.62). Small carvings, such as rosettes, are often held in a recess in a secondary jig, using double sided-tape (Fig 2.63). This jig can be held securely on the work station by any of the methods described above.

Fig 2.63 A small rosette blank held in a routed recess

Many woodcarvers who do small, detailed work often secure blanks to a slanted surface and sit at the bench or table. The view is then more perpendicular to the work and manipulation of the tools is easier, without the back strain associated with leaning over a bench. An easel can be made which fits snugly over the fences of the basic work station, as shown in Figs 2.64 and 2.65. Cut two 30–60–90° triangular ends from plywood; the hypotenuses are notched to fit over the fixed fences. These ends are connected by two plywood pieces, creating a 90° apex. The length is the same as the distance between the fixed end fences, plus an inch (25mm) or so either end to create a flange for clamping blanks to the top. If there is a little play in the length, wedges or filler strips can be used to secure the easel. The design offers a choice of two different slopes. If the blank does not reach from end to end of the easel, an auxiliary fence can be

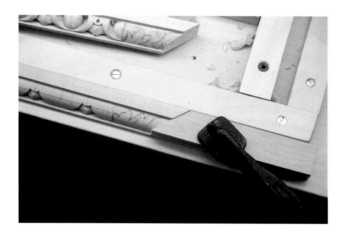

Fig 2.61 Mitered end of moulding being held by a mitered block on the lip of the work station

Fig 2.62 A length of moulding clamped by means of negative-profiled blocks

Fig 2.64 *End view of the easel, showing how it fits over the fences of the work station*

Fig 2.65 *At work on the easel*

screwed to the apex and used as an additional clamping flange. Much work may be secured by screwing from behind, as on the flat side of the basic work station. Instead of a plywood front, one could use a series of solid wood slats for the surface, spaced so that a clamp can be slipped through them. Clamping the blank to slats affords many quick and varied options.

PLANNING THE DESIGN

Many resources for traditional designs are available from publishers such as Dover Publications Inc., but every carver should practice sketching from nature. Most decorative work begins as a drawing, and a satisfactory design may require many revisions. If the design must fit into a defined area, first draw the perimeter mechanically. Over this, place a piece of tracing paper, and begin sketching the design. Remember the principles of design discussed in Chapter 1. To make revisions, overlay another sheet of tracing paper. After a few changes and a few smudges, the layers become confusing, so redraw the entire design and remove the earlier layers. This way one rehearses the design in the visual mind (Fig 2.66). Finally, transfer the design to the material using carbon paper, photocopy, or, if making multiples, a template.

THE PRELIMINARY MODEL

From the two-dimensional drawing one should be able to visualize the forms represented. As advocated in many woodcarving manuals, it is helpful to model them in clay. Though this technique is usually associated with sculpture, it is not uncommon to make models for relief work as well. In the apricot series of carvings one can readily see the progression from "drawn" incisions to the sculptural *alto-rilievo*; but in work requiring perspective as opposed to actual representation of mass, a clay model might be all the more necessary. Through modeling one understands mass and the relationship of planes. The model is only a sketch, and there should be no time spent on fussy details or textures. Revisions in clay are easy, and this saves endless hours of carving out design mistakes. Make the model and move on to the carving itself.

There are numerous plastic materials which may be used for modeling, such as hard wax, natural and synthetic clays, *papier mâché*, and synthetic modeling materials such as Plasticine, which are available from art-supply stores. Of these, I use Plasticine almost exclusively, though if one needs to present a model to a client a more permanent material such as clay should be used. Plasticine is cost-effective because it does not harden and is reusable. There are four grades of Plasticine in gray-green: #1 is soft, while #4 is hard. It is also available in white, grades #2 and #4. I store 10–15lb (4.5–7kg) of #2 gray-green in lidded plastic containers. Warm Plasticine is more workable than cold material, so put the container in the sun for a few minutes before modeling. Though the #2 grade does not droop, distortion inadvertently occurs as one works on adjacent areas. To make a model for molding and casting, a harder grade of material would be required.

Fig 2.66 Layers of tracing paper are used to "build up" a design, in this case the acanthus rinceau frieze shown complete in Fig 2.74

In addition to the "hands-on" manipulation, a variety of tools are used to shape the Plasticine. A large dowel can be used like a rolling pin to fabricate sheets, the ends carved to make scoops; a bevel-edged knife can be made quickly on a sander; smaller tools with tapers and paddle ends can be made from dowels. Working on a smooth surface such as laminate or glass prevents sticking and facilitates clean-up.

The process of modeling can be additive or subtractive, though the following description is in keeping with our theme of working from a two-dimensional drawing to the three-dimensional carving. On many-layered designs, the forms can be literally built up by placing the background levels down first, and those with most projection last. Some filler might have to be used to obtain the required three-dimensional appearance.

Fig 2.67 shows the model for the *mezzo-rilievo* version of the apricot design. Start by placing the **cartoon** under a piece of glass. For something similar to our apricot panel, fabricate the masses (fruits) separately by hand and roll out the planes (leaves) with rolling pin or dowel. Some shapes can be cut out with a wooden knife or a "cookie cutter" made from a tin can. Cans can be bent to make elliptical, **vesica piscis**, or even teardrop-shaped cutters. Then the leaves are rolled and cut. Short stems are attached to the leaves and fruit. The main twig is made by rolling the Plasticine between the hands, and then laid on the glass to conform to the curving twig of the cartoon. After placing the fruits on the glass and attaching them to

the main branch, the leaves are supported with Plasticine at the desired angles. The main branch is then raised in the middle so that it undulates in three dimensions.

Wood can be carved to thinner sections than Plasticine, so the model may look somewhat heavier than the final carving. Plasticine is also a flat, uniform color, while wood has grain which can add interest to the form. Experimentation and practice make this process both enjoyable and helpful. The subtraction process of modeling mimics the carving process, but is labor-intensive compared with the additive process just described. Of course, both methods are used in defining details.

Fig 2.67 A clay model for the apricot carving

CARVING THE DESIGN IN WOOD

After the design has been transferred to the blank, and the blank secured to the bench or work station, the first procedure is to isolate the mass of the carving from the background. This is called **bosting**, bosting-in, or wasting. The term is taken from the French *ébaucher*, to sketch. A large veiner or #9 gouge is used to make a groove around the design, ¹⁄₁₆in (1.5mm) or so from the outline. Outside this groove the material is wasted down close to the intended background level. In most cases this is a mechanical exercise, but it obviously determines the relationship of masses. It should be done with care, leaving the areas in question proud.

The outline of the design is then **set in**. Gouges are selected which coincide with the outline curves or lines of the design. The gouge is most often positioned vertically to the surface of the material and pressed down to create a vertical wall; the waste side of the material should fall away in a wedging action. For concave outlines the bevel of the blade pushes the tool outward toward this waste, making it hard to maintain a vertical wall; the tool can subsequently be tilted away from the work to create the verticality of the wall. For convex outlines the cannel or inside of the tool creates the vertical wall, the bevel pushing the waste away. Depending upon how much relief is intended, one may have to set in repeatedly around the outline. Care must be taken to use the same tool in the same location and to hold the tool at the same angle.

When setting-in is well along, a preliminary flattening of the background is done; this is **grounding**. A shallow gouge is used. A modified fishtail gouge (#2 Pfeil brand or #3 in the Sheffield numbering), with the wings rounded to make it look like a spoon, is handy for general grounding procedures—but particularly in tight areas or for cleaning up after undercutting, because it will cut diagonally (I hesitate to say "sideways"). This can also be turned over and used for convex modeling, to avoid the danger of scarring the work with a sharp-cornered tool.

For large amounts of grounding, a hand-held router can be used with efficiency: it wastes material quickly, gives a consistent depth, and can be fairly accurate in setting in the outline. (Computer-controlled or CNC routers, of course, can be extremely accurate.) Using a straight bit, start in the middle of large areas and work outward so there is always enough material left to support the router base. Figs 2.68 and 2.69 show the use of a router on a **rinceau** or acanthus scroll panel. The router may be used in this way on convex surfaces, but the router base must be kept as nearly tangential as possible; otherwise rocking may undercut the element you are setting in.

The frieze panel used here to illustrate relief carving is of griffins (or gryphons), affronted, guarding the fire of Apollo—a popular neoclassical motif associated with courage and vigilance.

The process of **modeling** is most enjoyable, because this is where the abstract forms begin to come alive and take on a character separate from the material itself. This stage comprises the rounding, rippling, curving, and sloping of the separate surfaces to make them distinct from

Fig 2.69 A closer view of the routed blank; the outlines have now been set in with gouges, and a start has been made on establishing the different levels

Fig 2.68 The acanthus rinceau frieze grounded out by means of the router

Fig 2.70 Modeling begun, some details redrawn

Fig 2.71 A further stage of modeling

Fig 2.72 The completed acanthus scroll

Fig 2.73 The completed griffin; note the incised carving of the further wing

their neighbors. The two-dimensional drawing now becomes a three-dimensional relief (Figs 2.70 and 2.71). The completed modeling of a portion of the acanthus scroll is shown in Fig 2.72, while the completed griffin is shown in Fig 2.73. Fig 2.74 is an overall view of the completed panel. A similar idea can be seen in Fig 2.75, which shows a **tablet** supported by a cherub or **putto** whose lower body metamorphoses into an acanthus scroll.

To further enhance the relief and minimize the vertical side walls formed at the setting-in stage, **undercutting** is often employed. This is cutting around the outline of the form so as to make it slope inwards toward the ground. Narrow parts, like the branch in Fig 2.49, may be completely freed from the background. Undercutting is not necessary in every carving: sometimes it may give a tentative quality to the forms, or create a disconnection from the surrounding context. It may also result in delicate areas which are vulnerable to breakage.

In carving panels one should remember that material is being removed from one side of the blank, and this may lead to warping. Allow a little extra material so that the back and any contiguous border can be flattened after carving is complete. The amount of warp depends upon a number of factors: the species, how the blank is cut (especially if there are large amounts of end grain), its original dryness or stability, how quickly material is removed, environmental conditions, and final finish.

Fig 2.75 An acanthus scroll originating from a cherub, Richmond, VA

Fig 2.74 The finished carving (photograph by Ron Hurst/Photoworks)

PREIVS

TABLETS AND CARTOUCHES

Scrolls • Lettering

The visual importance of having a moulding or raised border to define a surface upon which to carve lettering and other graphics has long been understood. Such frames lend an enhanced authority to the message or symbol, by setting it apart from everyday clutter or from the entirely practical structure of a building or piece of furniture. Carving these borders offers a wonderful opportunity to explore the design relationships between message and presentation, to model undulating and scrolling surfaces, and, of course, to practice the many motifs associated with them, such as garlands, drapery, and lettering.

> *The lyf so short,*
> *the craft so long to lerne*
>
> GEOFFREY CHAUCER,
> *THE PARLIAMENT OF FOWLS*

In ancient Greece the most common use of formal inscriptions (to judge from surviving artifacts) was on funerary or dedicatory monuments (*stelae*), for inventories of treasures kept in temples, and on pottery to identify the heroes and gods depicted. In most of these examples the lettering is incised on the flat surface of the stone (or painted, in the case of pottery), without ancillary embellishment. Memorials often had a temple-like frame called an **aedicule,** consisting of flanking columns, entablature, and pediment. But here again, lettering was incised directly into the flat surface of the plinth or architrave of this aedicule. There was little tendency to separate the inscription within its own frame.

Certainly by Roman times, however, inscriptions were separated from the other elements or surrounding surface by a simple border of mouldings (Fig 3.1). The rise in Roman Imperial exploits and the need to announce them popularized the use of these **tablets.** The arches of Titus (82 CE) and Septimius Severus (203 CE), both in Rome, are good examples (Fig 3.2). Renaissance and later examples, however, incorporate additional elements such as embellished mouldings, supporting consoles, drapery (Fig 3.3), garlands (Fig 3.4), and architectural features.

The **medallion** is a plaque with a round or oval border enclosing relief carving, usually a monogram, symbol, or portrait head. The raised border often consists of egg-and-dart moulding, a wreath of leaves, or similar ornamentation (Fig 3.5).

The **cartouche** can serve similar purposes to the tablet, but has an undulating quality both in outline and in surface. The French term *cartouche* is derived from the Latin *carta* or *charta*, meaning "paper", via the Italian *cartoccio*, meaning "scroll". The term **escutcheon** (also French-derived) is sometimes used interchangeably with "cartouche", but is more often associated with the shield or "device" (often lozenge-shaped) of heraldry, and therefore the similar-shaped plate around a keyhole. In simple forms, the cartouche literally appears to be an animal skin (parchment) whose extremities have curled up. This may not be its actual origin, but in all forms there is a series of scroll-like edges curling forward or back around a central area or field. The field is often oval, and is oriented either horizontally or vertically depending upon its use or location. Fig 3.6 illustrates a door panel with the cartouche oriented horizontally.

The tablet in Fig 3.7 is a hybrid between the tablet and the cartouche, having a rectangular field and a frame of mostly flat scrolls. When used in a purely decorative context, the field is usually left plain, but monograms, symbols (Fig 3.8), or heraldic devices are frequent additions. Unlike the tablet, the cartouche is generally not used for long lines of text. Interestingly, the rectangular outline around the hieroglyph for the Pharoah's name is called a cartouche, reinforcing the use of the form as an identifier. The cartouche is found in many decorative arts, from silverware, in which engraved monograms appear, to maps, upon which the scale, location, and cartographer's name are inscribed.

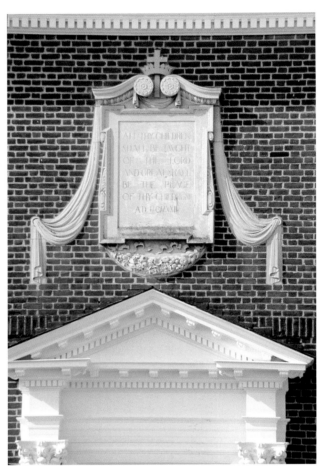

Fig 3.3 Crossetted tablet with scrolled pediment, drapery, and garland, surmounted by cross and crown symbols, Lynchburg, VA

Fig 3.1 Tablet in "rustic" lettering with moulded frame, in the Forum, Rome

Fig 3.2 Tablet on the Arch of Titus (82 CE), Rome

Fig 3.4 Tablet with pediment, fruit garland, and lions' heads, Library of Congress, Washington, DC

Fig 3.5 *Portrait medallion with egg-and-dart moulded frame, Vicenza, Italy*

Fig 3.6 *Door panel with cartouche oriented horizontally, Via D. Dataria, Rome*

Fig 3.7 *Hybrid tablet/cartouche, Piazza dei Signori, Verona, Italy*

Fig 3.8 *Cartouche with fleur-de-lis (the symbol of Florence), Santa Ornisanti, Florence, Italy*

In the Renaissance, the cartouche form is fully developed and often incorporates additional motifs such as shells (see Fig 3.8), masks (Fig 3.9), fanciful animals (Fig 3.10), cherubs (Fig 3.11), and, of course, foliage (Figs 3.12 and 3.13). Fig 3.14 shows a Baroque rendition, flamboyantly embellished and distorted, drooping between supporting consoles. In Fig 3.15 the cartouche frames an elliptical niche incorporating shells and a scrolled console pedestal for a bust (see Chapters 4 and 5, respectively). Many pattern books of the eighteenth century illustrate cartouches, keystones, urns, and the like; Fig 3.16 of memorial tablets by James Gibbs (1682–1754) shows the

Fig 3.9 *Masks incorporated into cartouche, Piazza Bra, Verona, Italy*

63

Fig 3.10 *Cartouche with monster resembling a bird of prey, Loggia dell'Orcagna, Florence*

Fig 3.11 *Cherub presenting the message, Verona, Italy*

Renaissance forms revived. The cartouche is not considered a strictly classical motif, however, and was therefore eschewed during subsequent neoclassical revivals.

The cartouche is mostly found in isolation, standing out from surrounding surfaces or other decoration. One does not see little cartouches strung along a moulding, but because they often carry identifiers, they occupy a central place in the overall scheme. When used in a tympanum, the cartouche (like the shell) is often flanked by flowing foliage to fill the space, as in Figs 3.13 and 3.17. Reinforcing the notion of centrality, keystones are often in cartouche form (see Figs 3.9 and 3.18, and Chapter 5). A keystone of this type is known as an **agrafe** or **agraffe**.

It is interesting to note the similarity between heraldic coats of arms and the cartouche. There was an integration of the two in northern Europe during the seventeenth and

Fig 3.12 *Cartouche on frieze band, flanked by acanthus rinceaux, Richmond, VA*

Fig 3.13 *In a tympanum, a cartouche with cornucopia, Staunton, VA*

Fig 3.14 Baroque
cartouche, Tribunale
Civile e Penale, Florence

Fig 3.17 Cartouche
with swirling foliage in
semicircular tympanum,
Verona, Italy

Fig 3.15 Cartouche-like
frame around elliptical
niche, Villa Borghese,
Rome

Fig 3.18 Keystone with
cartouche (agrafe),
interrupting or
"breaking" the horizontal
cornice of a pediment

Fig 3.16 Drawing by James
Gibbs, reproduced in Thomas
Arthur Strange, Antique
Furniture and Decorative
Accessories (by courtesy of
Dover Publications, Inc.)

Fig 3.19 Heraldic shield on cartouche, on a sarcophagus in the churchyard of Bruton Parish Church, Colonial Williamsburg, VA

eighteenth centuries, the coat of arms being surrounded by the cartouche. The two forms are depicted together, for example, on a tombstone at Bruton Parish Church, Colonial Williamsburg, VA (Fig 3.19). Indeed, the coat of arms might be considered a special sort of tablet or cartouche: it has an easily recognizable shield shape and depicts a signature, using pictorial symbols, colors, and geometric shapes. It did not originate as architectural ornament—it derives from medieval armor and the need for identification in battle—but has been subsequently incorporated into its decorative vocabulary. There are many distinctive shield shapes and different accouterments associated with them, such as helmets with mantles, supporters (Fig 3.20), and mottoes on banners. Though the pictorial or "device" upon the shield itself became strictly codified, involving particular terminology and hereditary protocols, in architectural decoration the shield is often left plain (Fig 3.21). Although some cartouches proper bear arms, we will not directly address the vast subject of heraldry here.

Fig 3.20 Royal coat of arms supported by a lion, Governor's Palace, Colonial Williamsburg, VA

Fig 3.21 Unadorned shield with foliage, London

TABLETS

As we have seen in Figs 3.3 and 3.4, the tablet can be embellished by a variety of ornamentation, such as drapery or garlands. It can have an architectural frame of **crossetted** architraves (Fig 3.22). (The term *crossetted* denotes the "overrun" or projection of one or both frame members beyond the adjoining one.) It can have an entablature or pediment above (as in Figs 3.3 and 3.4), or be supported by **ancons** (scrolled console blocks). The door panel in the Vatican (Fig 3.23) shows a tablet within a tablet: the bolection moulding of the panel acts as a frame for the whole carving, while the cherubs within hold up another tablet. In a sense, any "picture frame" which

Fig 3.23 A panel within which cherubs are holding an inscribed tablet (photograph by F. Wilbur used by permission of the Vatican Museums)

holds a panel with lettering could be considered a tablet. The mouldings can be of many varieties and in many different combinations, the carving of which is explained in my earlier book *Carving Architectural Detail in Wood*.

C- AND S-SCROLLS

C- and S-scrolls, which are essentially two-dimensional, provide the carver with a useful introduction to the three-dimensional complexities of the cartouche. In order to be successful they must have thickness, and must throw shadows for the sake of visual clarity. As the detail in Fig 3.24 shows, the section consists of a rounded convex profile with an opposite concavity or cove, which meet in a sharp **arris** or corner. The cove also contributes to the appearance of a spiral, the concave side giving way to the convexity as it curls around itself. Usually the overall flow is gentle, the C-scroll being only a segment of a circle,

Fig 3.22 Crossetted tablet with polychromed coat of arms, Via del Quirinale, Rome

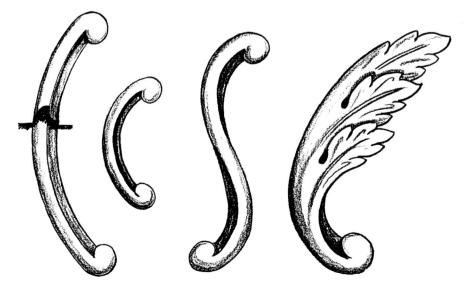

Fig 3.24 Several variations of the C- and S-scrolls

Fig 3.25 Symmetrical C-scrolls on a table apron, mid-20th century

rarely semicircular. It should be drawn by hand to avoid a stilted or mechanical look. There is no standard ratio of body width to head diameter, but only what fits the situation or the style. The S-scroll is an elongated form and rarely has the semicircular look of a Roman letter S.

Though these forms are introduced here to illustrate how to carve cartouche scrolls, they are frequently used two-dimensionally to define borders, such as along the aprons and chair rails of eighteenth-century furniture (see Figs 4.11 and 4.12 on page 88). The simplest version of the cartouche is the symmetrical C-scroll often found on the knees of eighteenth-century furniture, or in a central position on a side-table apron (Fig 3.25), on picture frames, and even as "keystones" (Fig 3.26). Combinations of C- and S-scrolls can be used to enclose a field for a monogram, house number, or other incised graphic, or as a self-contained ornament (Figs 3.27 and 3.28). These simple shapes can also be combined with other elements, such as foliage which flows from the spiral, or shells, cherubs, and so forth.

Fig 3.27 A flat, self-contained decorative arrangement of C-scrolls

Fig 3.26 "Keystone" or cresting in the form of a cartouche. The C-scrolls are canted toward the viewer and are therefore more three-dimensional than usual—an example of transition between the flat C-scroll and the volute of the cartouche proper

Fig 3.28 C-scrolls oriented back to back on a decorative plaque

These C- and S-scrolls are carved as any other relief would be: the shapes are bosted, set in, grounded, and then modeled. The "body" or long curve of the scroll is set in with shallow gouges which match the curvature. Each end consists of two semicircles (see Fig 3.24): the first defines the end of the main curve, while the second directs the curve inward. Ideally, then, two semicircular gouges can be used to define the shape, but in practice a slightly shallower sweep works better. I tend to use #7 gouges, being careful to match curves and to "track" the tool so that the transition from one semicircle to the other is smooth. Usually the diameter of the end exceeds the width of the body of the scroll, which is uniform. The inner, coved profile of the body meets the convexity as it forms the head of the scroll; the cove will be about half the diameter of the smaller semicircle which carries the spiral inward. The arris between cove and convexity should parallel the two outside edges. As you can see by studying the photographs, there are as many exceptions as there are general characteristics. Fig 3.29 shows symmetrical C-scrolls head to head, framing an elliptical ground with initial.

In the S-scroll, the cove becomes shallower, or tapers, as it approaches (and passes) the longitudinal midpoint where the body curve reverses. The middle convexity should not appear too heavy or thick.

Fig 3.29 C-scroll cartouche with initial

CARVING A C- AND S-SCROLL CARTOUCHE

A combination of C- and S-scrolls, a few sprigs of foliage, and a shell lends interest to the cartouche in Fig 3.30. Because this design will be used for a name or house number in a single horizontal line (see Fig 7.2 on page 142), it resembles the hybrid tablet of Fig 3.7 in its two-dimensional scrolling. The thickness of the various scrolls should be similar; those with foliage may tend to appear heavier, and should be adjusted to avoid this. The relative weights of the various elements should always balance:

Fig 3.30 A design for a cartouche of C- and S-scrolls

the delicacy or boldness of the scrolls should support the detail of the leaves or shell, or any other added ornament. It is preferable to avoid lines which bulge out here or appear thin-waisted there; the sizes as well as the curves of each element should complement each other. The silhouette should flow evenly (disregarding the knobby "heads" of the scrolls).

The blank is bandsawn and trued up, and the area inside the border is bosted or wasted with a large veiner or #9 gouge. Instead of taking the entire ground to the same flat level, however, the center is allowed to remain near the surface to create a gently domed field. A depth gauge of some sort will help to keep the scrolls to an even depth and thickness; the gauge pictured in Fig 3.31 is made from a scrap piece of wood with a shallow groove in which a pencil is held by a screw and a fender washer. The shell to the exterior of the scrolls is lowered somewhat to provide clearance.

After creating the raised border containing the scrolls, the convex edges of the scrolls are carved first and their ends rounded (Fig 3.32). The spiral of each scroll end is stabbed in, and this serves as a stop cut for the ensuing cutting of the cove (Fig 3.33). Remember that the sharp arris between the convex edge and interior cove should parallel the side of the scroll. This does not apply to the S-scroll, where the coves taper as they approach the mid-point of the scroll (Fig 3.34).

The outline of the foliage is set in like any relief carving. From the rounded outside edge, the leaf surface takes on a gentle curve to the ends of the leaves at the inside of the cartouche. The shell-like form added to the silhouette is carved last. It has a scalloped outline

Fig 3.32 Rounding over the scroll head with the gouge bevel-up

Fig 3.33 Carving the cove as it meets the head of the scroll

Fig 3.31 Using a shop-made depth gauge to ensure evenness of field depth, and therefore even thickness of the bordering scrolls

Fig 3.34 The completed S-scroll, showing how the concavity fades out toward the middle of the body

Fig 3.35 The scrolled cartouche complete and ready for painting (cf. Fig 7.2, page 142)

with flutes radiating from a central point; like all flutes, these increase in size as they reach the outer edge, necessitating the use of several different-sized tools. (There is more on carving shells in Chapter 4.) Fig 3.35 shows the completed cartouche.

To make the transition from the two-dimensional C-scroll to the three-dimensional volute of the cartouche, it is necessary to slope or cant the spiral end of the scroll, while continuing the spiral inward for a few more turns. The progression can be seen by comparing Figs 3.36 or 3.28 with the transitional examples in Figs 3.37 or 3.26,

and finally with Figs 3.8 or 3.20, which depict high-relief volutes. This makes the scroll more readable: the cove, instead of butting against the semicircle, now follows it inward, albeit on a steeper incline. (The term **volute** is used for deep-relief spirals, but is usually reserved for those of Ionic and Corinthian capitals, and for consoles.) The more the end is sloped (the more perpendicular it is with the face of the roll), the more like a curled parchment it becomes. In the case of the double-ended roll found on fully developed cartouches, the actual surface, if one could uncurl it, would be a dovetail shape.

Fig 3.36 A cartouche of simple, flat scrolls

Fig 3.37 Cartouche with C-scrolls canted from the background—the beginnings of a volute

CARVING A TRANSITIONAL TABLET/CARTOUCHE

This hybrid between tablet and cartouche shows several different scroll-end configurations (Fig 3.38). Placing the rectangular tablet over the more fluid surround of scrolling decoration presents an opportunity to carve scrolls in high relief . In Fig 3.39 the interior surface of the tablet has been lowered so that the scrolls are isolated and can be carved in high relief. Material is left at either side for the floral drops, and at the bottom for the scroll. After some work has been done, a depth gauge will be helpful to ensure that the ground is parallel to the back of the blank. A "pointing" apparatus can be made from several scrap pieces and dowels (Fig 3.40). A collar adjusts along the vertical dowel (which has been fixed to a small plywood base) and is held by a bolt in a threaded insert. This collar also has a hole to house the horizontally adjustable arm. A saw kerf is cut into the hole so that a small bolt can pinch the arm tightly. The pointer fits snugly into a hole drilled in the arm. This device serves to transfer a location relative to the back of the blank (or the face of the plywood upon which it is mounted) to various points on the surface of the recess. This is the same as the pointing system used by sculptors to transfer measurements from a clay or plaster model to the work.

Another handy device is a parallel rule for quickly drawing parallel lines, setting out guidelines for lettering, and checking the symmetry of elements. It consists of two parallel-sided bars of any length, and two connecting arms which swivel on equally spaced pivots (Fig 3.41). Accuracy in drilling the holes and sizing the pivots (bolts in this case) can be achieved by clamping or taping the bars together and drilling both at the same time. Then

Fig 3.39 *The scrolls isolated from the ground*

Fig 3.40 *A pointer depth gauge to ensure even depth*

drill the arms in the same way. One can purchase parallel rules of this type: I have seen both 6in (152mm) and 12in (305mm) versions at antique tool shows.

When the rectangular tablet area has been lowered just enough to accommodate the top roll, set in the rectangular tablet and relieve the surrounding area to

Fig 3.38 *A transitional tablet/cartouche with fully developed volutes, floral drops, and shell*

the final cartouche depth. The roll should be about as deep as it is wide; you will probably want to round the roll first in order to determine this depth. After isolating the roll and setting in the round of the end, begin the slope from the ground up toward the spiral (Fig 3.42). Because in this example I wanted high relief and definite separation between the curls, I did not slope the whole end of the roll first, as I would for a simpler version. My approach was to isolate the extent of each curl and slope the edges as I worked the curls, so that the inner curl projects more than the outer one. (Fig 3.49 shows the result viewed from a low angle.) Begin by sloping the ground into the roll end, and when you come to the straight line denoting the surface of the next layer (or curl), set in a straight line using a chisel (Fig 3.43). Then continue to set in the curve of the outer layer (Fig 3.44). Approaching the bottom edge, remember to allow for the thickness

Fig 3.43 *Setting in the straight line of the roll on the surface of the scroll*

Fig 3.41 *A shop-made parallel rule can be used to compare elements or measurements, or to draw parallel lines for lettering*

Fig 3.44 *Setting in the curving edge of the scroll with an appropriate gouge*

Fig 3.42 *The top scroll isolated from the background; the upward slope of the end has been started*

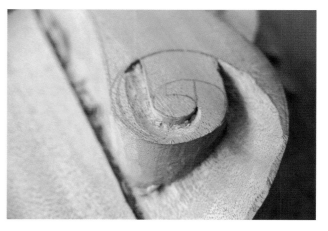

Fig 3.45 *The inner roll has been isolated by relieving the adjoining area*

Fig 3.46 Continuing to work around the scroll

of the material (Fig 3.45). Set in the second straight line and round the end of the next layer, relieving as you go. It helps to make sense of the curves if you begin the rounding of the whole roll and slope the edges, as has been done in Figs 3.46 and 3.47.

If you have trouble visualizing the layers of the curls, it might be worthwhile to cut a paper trapezoid and roll it around a dowel, starting from its base or wide side. The inner curls will project further than the outer ones.

The next stage is to undercut the scroll edges (Fig 3.48). Fig 3.49 shows the side view of the scroll and how the inner curls project beyond the outer ones. Looking perpendicular to the end slope reveals slight distortion (Fig 3.50), but in Fig 3.51, which shows the front elevation looking slightly upward—the way it would usually be seen—the spiral appears a little more true. The backward curls of the end ribbons are accomplished in similar fashion; Fig 3.52 shows the last stages of undercutting.

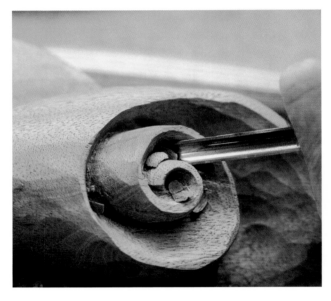

Fig 3.48 Undercutting and thinning the scroll walls

Fig 3.47 The scroll has been roughed out and its layers defined

Fig 3.49 The scroll end viewed from a low angle to show how the successive layers project

Fig 3.50 The finished scroll end seen straight on

Fig 3.51 The finished scroll seen from the normal viewing position

After the floral drops, scrolls, and shell have been carved, the field should be flattened with a shallow gouge and scraper (Fig 3.53) so that the fillet of the tablet moulding will be even. To prepare the field for lettering, it should again be scraped smooth after the moulding has been carved; it is extremely difficult to incise nice-looking letters on a rough or undulating surface.

Once the lettering is complete, the back edges of the entire tablet are relieved or back-cut. To hold and protect the carved tablet while doing this, a piece of waffle rubber rug mat can be used (Fig 3.54). Attach the ends of the padding—about 36in (90cm) long and a little narrower than the width of the bench—to battens which are long enough to be clamped across the bench. Wrap the padding around the battens as close to the length of the carving as possible, and clamp the battens to the bench so that they act as fences (Fig 3.55). Towels or other padding placed here and there will help prevent rocking.

Fig 3.52 Carving the ribbons at either side of the tablet

Fig 3.53 Using a scraper to flatten the ground for the rectangular frame. The same process will be used to level the ground of the inner tablet for lettering

Fig 3.54 Using an anti-slip rubber mat with fences to hold and protect the tablet while undercutting or back-cutting

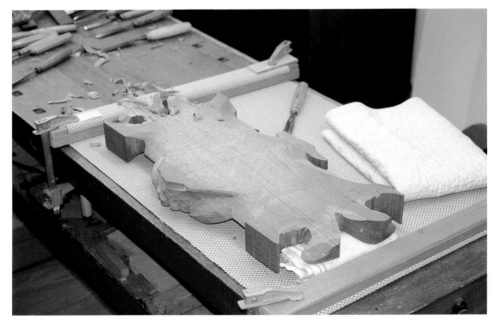

Fig 3.55 A detail showing the construction of the cleats which hold the mat

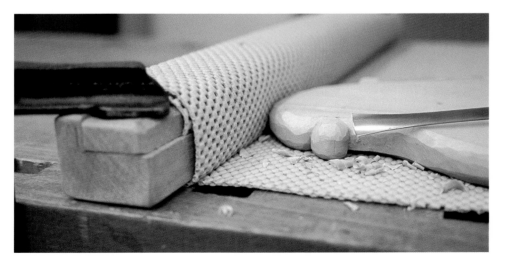

LETTERING

In *The Art of Hand Lettering*, Helm Wotzkow explains that there are five qualities of good lettering which can be evaluated: size, form, weight, spacing, and execution. Though Wotzkow is concerned with calligraphy, not typography, these aspects of lettering apply to carved letters as well. The following synopsis is derived from his lucid explanations.

- *Size* is defined by the relationship between the lettering and its environment, including such things as the surrounding surface, carved borders, and other embellishments, as well as the distance from which it is read.
- *Form* refers to the style of the lettering, including the shapes of the individual letters, and the appropriateness of the style to the subject matter or intention of the message.
- *Weight* concerns the thickness of the strokes making up the letters, relative to each other and the plain surface around them.
- *Layout* is the general composition and its effectiveness in obtaining a pleasing or striking result.
- *Spacing*, though it seems an obvious concern, is complicated by the fact that it includes letter-to-letter spacing, word spacing, and line spacing.
- Finally, *execution* deals with the actual precision of making or writing the letter.

Though they may be considered separately for discussion purposes, there is a dependent relationship among these five qualities. A noticeable change in weight may alter the form or the implication of the message, for instance.

As we are concerned with classical decorative elements, it is apropos to restrict our discussion of lettering to the Roman majuscules or upper-case letters (Fig 3.56). (See also Fig 3.2 on page 62.) Despite the Renaissance interest in classical arts and letters, as well as the need for some standardization in the formative years of typography, "the construction of roman capitals in absolute conformity with classical precedents is exceptional" (Stanley Morison, *Pacioli's Classic Roman Alphabet*, p. 78). For instance, the Roman E had all three horizontal bars of even length and the S was quite narrow, but changing sensibilities altered these letters to make them more consistent with the others. A number of scholars and artists in the Renaissance proposed ways of constructing letters geometrically. Sebastiano Serlio (1475–1554) in his *Five Books of Architecture* mentions the work of several pre-decessors (Dover Publications Inc. has reproduced the alphabets of both Luca Pacioli and Albrecht Dürer) and illustrates the usual method of inscribing letters within a square (Fig 3.57).

It is generally accepted that the letter O is very close to a circle, which, of course, can be inscribed within a square. This unit can be considered the basis for determining the proportions of the other letters. With some very subtle exceptions, all letters can be assumed to be the same height and, as can be observed, many of Serlio's letters are as wide overall as they are tall. Some, like the B, E, F, K, P, and T, are about three-quarters width, while others, like C, S, and I, vary from the basic unit. There are a number of calligraphic subtleties which are designed to counter the illusion that some letters are shorter than others. For example, the O extends above and below the height guidelines, and the apex of the A extends above the guideline.

Fig 3.56 Roman lettering, the Forum, Rome

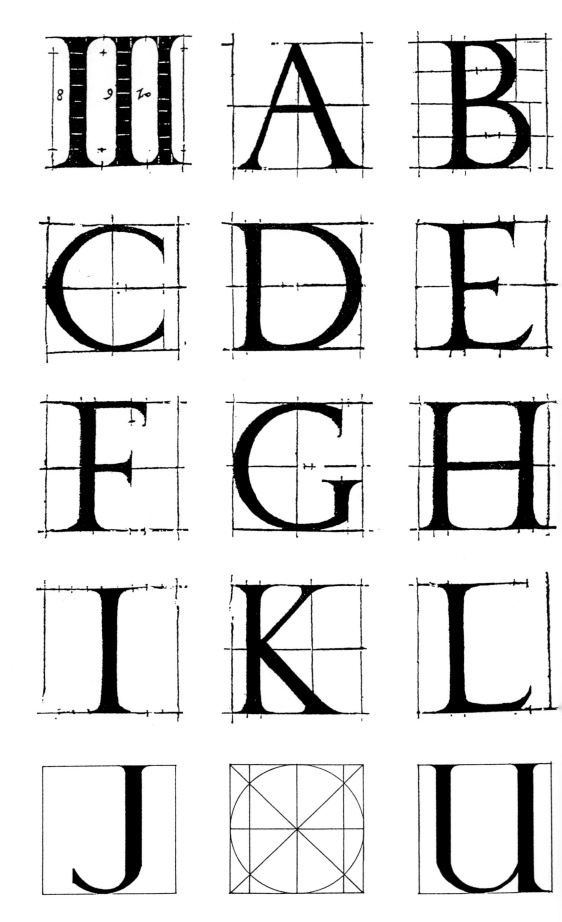

Fig 3.57 Roman alphabet from Serlio, The Five Books of Architecture *(by courtesy of Dover Publications, Inc.), with modern J, U, and W added for completeness*

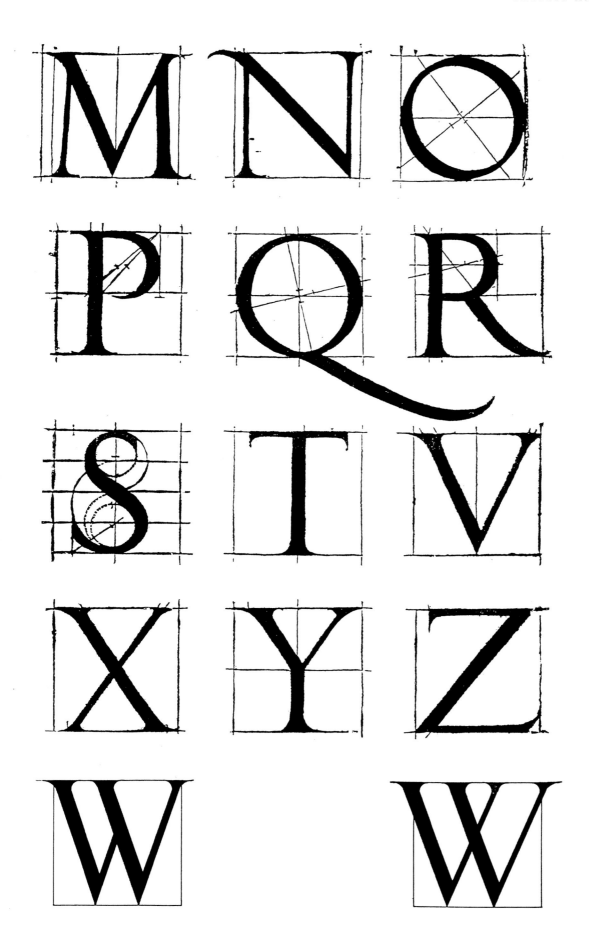

One way to approximate the three-quarters width is to draw a circle within a square, and draw the diagonals of the square. Then draw two vertical lines through the points of intersection between the diagonals and the circle, as shown on page 78, bottom center.

At the beginning of Fig 3.57, Serlio has shown the relationship between the thickness of the stroke and the height, the "bolder" letter having a thickness equal to ⅛ of the side of the square, and the "lighter" ¹⁄₁₀. The rest of his examples use the median width of ⅑. These are not the same as the old Roman *scriptura monumentalis*, however. One example already mentioned is the E, whose horizontal bars, originally equal in length, are given uneven length, with the bottom one longest. Because the Roman alphabet did not include J, U, and W, I have appended these to Serlio's letters. W has several variations: Serlio did not have to justify cramming it into a square! The body of my first W fits into the square, but the serifs extend about ⅑ wider. The second example, made of overlapping Vs, is considerably wider than the other letters.

The spaces between letters are not the same, and should be adjusted so that they appear to be equal in weight. One way to test this is to shade the spaces between letters, close one eye, and see whether the dark areas are equal. Letters with vertical strokes in juxtaposition (MILL, for instance) will be further apart than those with rounded forms (DOG), which almost touch one another. In the word SPACE, the round part of the P may actually overlap the foot of the A. Err to the generous side when laying out margins. One can get caught up in the geometrical exactness of the letters, figuring degrees of the angles, centers for the arcs, and so forth, but "in fact, where plume- or brush-written letters are used, small technical imperfections, if purely incidental, can often enhance and emphasize the beauty and character of the lettering" (Wotzkow, p. 27).

There is no need to spend hours perfecting one's calligraphic skills, but having a good alphabet ready to hand will continually assist in producing acceptable lettering. A sheet that can be enlarged or reduced on a photocopy machine is helpful; you can then trace from this master sheet. Co-ordinate the size of the lettering with the available space, and photocopy the master sheet close to this size. Rule a piece of tracing paper to this height, place it over the first letter needed, and trace it. Replace the paper over the next letter required, paying attention to proper spacing. When one line is complete, place the tracing paper over a blank piece of white paper and examine the spacing. In this way a pattern is built up ready to be transferred to the work. Carbon paper works well for this, but re-examine the result once the lettering has been transferred. Use a transparent plastic ruler and square to tidy up. One trick to spacing while using this method is to begin in the middle of the word or line, especially if there is an A near the middle. This is one of the problem letters, because it creates a lot of space at the top while having "big feet". Then work either side toward the beginning and end of the word or line.

This may seem like a restrictive, mechanical method, but for those who do not carve lettering frequently it is efficient and does not require lots of practice. There are, of course, computer programs which will allow you to modify and arrange many different letter fonts.

MONOGRAMS

Monograms, which often appear on cartouches as in Fig 3.58, are a combination of letters assembled into a single device. The letters usually overlap or entwine, parts of the letters or serifs are sometimes exaggerated to balance the composition, and occasionally letters are actually reversed to achieve symmetry. Some monogram resource books are listed in the Select Bibliography.

Monograms with relief letters that overlap can be carved as such, but incised letters present a potential problem in readability. There are two possible solutions. The stroke passing "under" another can be stopped a small distance from the "over" stroke, almost like thread

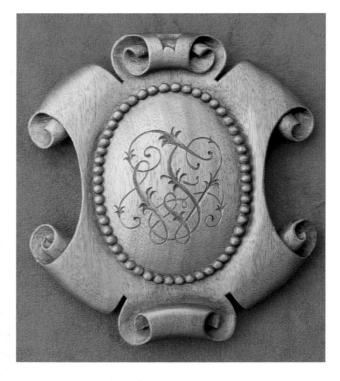

Fig 3.58 A cartouche with FW monogram

diving into the fabric. Alternatively, the overlapping lines can simply run into each other, as in Fig 3.58. This works best when the various elements differ significantly in width, so that the narrow lines, being less deep, do not interrupt the side walls of the wider strokes too much.

In carving letters, I generally follow the traditional method which matches the sweep of the gouge to the letter's outline. Assuming the grain is perpendicular to the vertical strokes, I start with these first, setting in a centerline stop-cut using either a bench chisel or a carver's chisel. I then make the opposing angled cuts to create the valley of the letter. An angle of 50–60° makes the valley deep enough to cast a strong shadow. The thinner, shallower elements will also produce effective shadows at this angle. When the lettering is to be gilded, I generally make it a little less deep: the gilding is easier and also tends to reflect light more effectively.

Once the straight members are finished, I use a fishtail chisel to cut the sloping end of the vertical stroke and to round the transitions between serifs and straight members. I do the curved elements last. On curved members I use the usual method of setting in a center stop-cut, then using matched sweeps to outline the outer curve. I use a shearing cut with a fishtail chisel on the interior of the curve. This usually requires shearing from two directions to avoid grain tear-out. Cleaning up transitions or smoothing long curves is done with the chisel used bevel-down to act like a plane. In fact, on continuous curves such as the S, I use the chisel for the body of the letter.

CARVING THE MONOGRAMMED CARTOUCHE

The cartouche already seen in Fig 3.58 is a typical example, with the oval field oriented vertically. The two side scrolls curl backward, while scrolls to top and bottom both curl forward. To add a little interest, the domed field is bordered by a ring of beads, and the top scroll has been cut away in the middle to emphasize the notion that it surely curls under. The letters, carved with a parting tool and smaller gouges, are about 3½in (90mm) tall.

After developing a satisfactory drawing, lay it out on the blank with the grain oriented vertically. Attempt to establish the desired section through the vertical centerline in order to determine the proper thickness of the blank; it is always prudent to begin with a blank a little thicker than predicted. (In the event, the blank shown in this sequence turned out to be too thick for the scrolls I wanted to carve; the extra material was removed with the bandsaw after carving of the cartouche was complete, and before back-cutting.)

An efficient way to check the symmetry of the bandsawn blank is to use a compass with its fixed leg on the centerline and swing it from side to side. Another way is to use an Omnigrid®, which is a piece of clear plastic with a centerline and gridlines printed on it at intervals of ⅛in (3mm), making visual comparisons easy and accurate (Fig 3.59). This is a tool borrowed from quilters, and is available at sewing supply stores.

Fig 3.59 The bandsawn blank screwed to a backing board, with the Omnigrid® in place to check the accuracy of the pattern transfer

Begin by bosting and setting in the oval defining the outside line of the beads. Relieving the outside of this oval should be done close to the outline so as not to interfere with the top and bottom scrolls. Even the side scrolls rise quickly from the field. Measure the depth frequently to ensure that the valley is taken down evenly around the oval. Alternatively, work the field down with a flat chisel or with a shallow gouge turned over, so that the vertical wall of the oval is about as thick as the intended diameter of the beads (Fig 3.60 shows the step or flat at the perimeter of the oval which will become the bead ring).

In this example, the projection at the center of the field is close to the original surface—the same as the furthest projection of the top and bottom scrolls. The rest of the field is taken down further, to give the impression of being "framed" by the surrounding scrolls, so that the ring of beads is actually below the center of the field. If helpful, a preliminary trench can be made to isolate the area of the beads. The width of the encircling beads can be redrawn using a compass, by partly retracting the pencil so that the fixed leg will rub the oval (Fig 3.60). After setting in the interior line for the beads, the field will have

Fig 3.60 Marking the elliptical astragal, which will eventually become a ring of beads

Fig 3.61 Using a backbent gouge to round the astragal

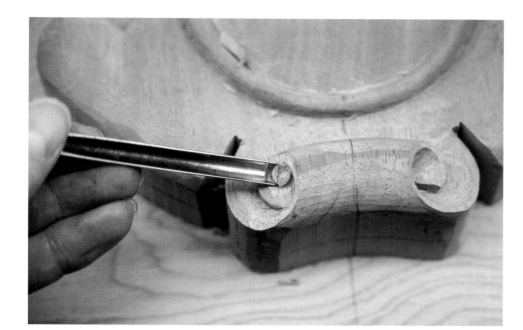

Fig 3.62 Relieving the scroll

Fig 3.63 Sighting from the side to check for symmetry in the slope of the roll end

to be taken down further to raise the ring. The ring is then rounded over to make an astragal (half-round) profile; a backbent tool is handy here (Fig 3.61). Wait until the other carving is done before forming the individual beads.

Block out the top and bottom scrolls, and round the outer edges of the side scrolls. Reduce the top and bottom scrolls to half-round rolls. Carve the scrolls in a similar fashion to those of the transitional tablet previously explained. The process is similar to creating simulated folds, as on **linenfold** panels. Fig 3.62 shows the bottom scroll nearing completion. Fig 3.63 shows inspection of the scroll to determine that the slopes are symmetrical.

Once the scrolls are finished, carve the beads around the field. These are laid out symmetrically, using the axes. They are more difficult to carve on a curve than in a straight line, because of the change in orientation of the grain.

Undercutting is started while the cartouche is still on the bench, but visibility can be improved by placing it in a vise while it is still screwed to the work station or backboard.

The monogram on my cartouche is distinctly non-Roman in character: a fluid rendering of F and W. Notice how the overall composition appears balanced in spite of the asymmetrical treatment of the letters, which have extended flourishes or *swashes*.

DETAIL AT CLERGY CHAIR

26

A B

④ PROFILE DETAIL
F-7   6"=1'-0"

RADIATING DESIGNS

Fans • Sunbursts • Shells

The one common feature of the elements discussed in this chapter is that the flutes or valleys composing the design widen as they radiate from a central point. The technique is to use a series of related gouges to produce a smooth expansion of the basic geometric shape. The cross section of the flute or valley should remain the same proportionally throughout its extent.

A PRACTICAL EXERCISE

If you are not sure which gouges will produce the desired flute, it is worth taking the time to practice on a scrap piece of material. Begin by simply drawing two straight lines across the grain. Do not make the two lines parallel: the distance between them at the wide end should be less than the thickness of the wood, and the narrow end should be half the width of the wide end. Begin with a narrow #9 gouge which just about matches the narrowest width; make a groove between the lines, starting at the narrow end. As you work the narrow end down to final depth, it becomes clear that there is only one place along the flute (think of it as a truncated half-cone) where gouge and desired profile match; this would be at or near the edge of the board with the narrow #9 gouge. You will need to use the wings of the gouge to widen the flute enough for the next larger gouge to be inserted. (You cannot start at the wide end with a gouge that matches, because it would immediately dig into the diminishing sides of the flute.) The groove made should be semicircular. Depending upon the actual situation (on the grain direction or the proximity of other elements, for example), you may need to work the flute

> To attempt to build up theories of art, or to form a style independently of the past, would be an act of supreme folly.
>
> OWEN JONES,
> THE GRAMMAR OF ORNAMENT

from both directions, but the principle is the same. It is easier to work from the narrow area toward the wider one. Either way, it may be helpful to work the transitions of the flute side walls with a slightly shallower #8 gouge, or with the wings of a #11 veiner.

TYPES OF RADIATING MOTIF

The shell is among the motifs which are pervasive throughout Western art. Among the many elements I have carved, the shell is one of the more satisfying, and commissions which involve them seldom disappoint me. From the simple spandrel fans and sunbursts often associated with American Federal mantelpieces, to the pediment shell with foliage or the niche shell, radiating designs demand method and care. The curves are aesthetically pleasing—a mystery akin to the attraction of the golden ratio, perhaps.

Flower **rosettes**, consisting of a central disk and radiating petals, sepals, and/or leaves, are probably the most common radiating design. They are found on the metopes of the Doric frieze, between the modillions of the Corinthian Order, and in the coffers of a vault. They are also found on mantelpieces, picture frames, and furniture, and wherever a square or oblong area would otherwise look too plain. See my *Carving Architectural Detail in Wood* for further discussion.

The **fan** is a geometric design described by a semicircle or quarter-circle, having radiating peaks and valleys, flutes, or convex reeds. (I use "reeds" here for lack of a better term: it usually refers to parallel rather than radiating half-round mouldings.) Fans are usually carved into the surface of the wood but, as the door panel in Fig 4.1 shows, they may be in relief. The fan is the simplest of the radiating designs, with rarely any embellishment.

The semicircular fan is usually found in a central position, as in a pediment (Fig 4.2) or a drawer front. The quarter-fan, on the other hand, is normally relegated to the corners of a surface or structure; Fig 4.3 shows a peak-and-valley corner fan in cast iron. A similar location is the spandrel of an arch, but in this instance the outside perimeter is turned inside-out as it were, the extremity following the curve of the arc; Fig 4.4 shows a bookcase head with spandrel flutes (see also Fig 2.17 on page 38).

The **sunburst** is similar to the fan, but usually round or elliptical in shape, with the individual elements radiating flutes, peaks, or reeds (Figs 4.5 and 4.6).

Other radiating designs include the depiction of the sun surrounded by narrow rays, or alternating straight and wavy rays. Such rays emanating from the heads of gods and holy personages are an ancient association. The **Apolline** ornament shows Apollo as sun god (Fig 4.7). Sacred symbols with associated rays are also used in

Fig 4.3 Corner fan of peak-and-valley type on a cast-iron store front, Rocky Mount, NC

Fig 4.4 Spandrel flutes on a bookcase head, shown here before installation

Fig 4.1 Door panel with simple semicircular fan, Florence, Italy

Fig 4.2 Dormer window with fan in pediment; note the keystone and finial above. Lynchburg, VA

Christianity (Fig 4.8): rays are ubiquitous in depictions of Christ and family, the Apostles, the saints, and the Holy Spirit (which is often represented by wings or a dove).

There are also hybrids which combine elements of fan or sunburst with features of the shell. The drawer front in Fig 4.9 does not have flutes like a typical shell, yet it has a generally concave section. The background to the symbol of Florence in Fig 4.10 is similar to a shell, but circular.

The use of the shells of bivalve mollusks as decorative motifs may have multiple origins. From ancient times shells were, naturally, associated with the sea and the sea god Poseidon, and also with legends concerning the marine birth of Aphrodite (Venus), later depicted by Botticelli. Christian pilgrims from the twelfth century onwards (including Chaucer's Wife of Bath) wore the scallop shell

Fig 4.5 *Sunbursts in a frieze, Philadelphia, PA*

Fig 4.6 *Sunburst oriented vertically on a pilaster, Staunton, VA*

Fig 4.7 *Apolline representation, University of Virginia, Charlottesville, VA*

Fig 4.8 *The pedimental carving on S. Giovannino degli Scoplopi (1579) in Florence, Italy, shows the use of sun rays to symbolize spiritual presence*

Fig 4.9 *Lowboy drawer front with design transitional between fan and shell (by courtesy of Mrs Robert L. Wilbur)*

The Philadelphia lowboy in Fig 4.11 shows both a drawer shell with foliage and an apron shell flanked by C-scrolls. Fig 4.12 is a close-up of the same piece. Fig 7.56 on page 163 shows a further example. In architecture, the shell shows up on pediments (Fig 4.13), friezes (Fig 4.14), and even pilaster capitals (Fig 4.15).

Shells may also form the quadrant sphere in niches and corner cabinets. The niche in Fig 4.16 shows the hinge oriented at the top of the arch, but it is more common to find it at the bottom as in Fig 4.17.

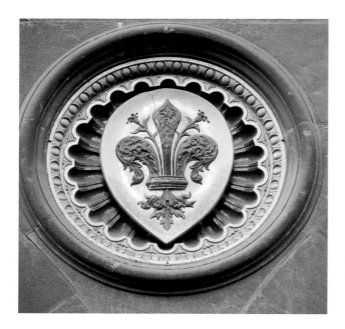

Fig 4.10 The symbol of Florence on the Poste Centrale, showing the shell-like circular background

as a symbol that they had completed the pilgrimage to the Shrine of St James of Compostela in Spain. It became a pervasive decorative element in the later seventeenth and early eighteenth centuries, showing up on everything from silverware and porcelain to furniture.

As for furniture, the shell was carved into the aprons, crest rails, and knees of chairs, and on the drawer fronts of case pieces and Goddard-Townsend block-front desks.

Fig 4.12 Detail of the Philadelphia lowboy (photograph by courtesy of Todd D. Prickett)

Fig 4.11 Philadelphia lowboy, c.1775, showing two varieties of shell. The drawer front has a reverse or concave shell formed of elongated leaves with lightly scrolled ends. The apron shell is similar to the obverse shell described in the text. Note the C- and S-scrolls along the edge of the apron (owned by C. L. Prickett; photograph by courtesy of Todd D. Prickett)

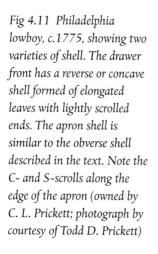

Fig 4.13 *Shell in open segmental pediment, Florence, Italy*

Fig 4.14 *Flanked by scrolling foliage, the shell is central on this entablature frieze in Florence*

Fig 4.15 *Shell on pilaster capital, Vicenza, Italy*

Fig 4.16 *Niche shell with hinge at top, Rome, Italy*

Fig 4.17 *The more common orientation of niche shell, Rome*

CARVING THE FAN

The layout of fan designs is straightforward, as they are based on the circle, and each division has the same number of degrees. Half-units on the straight sides, as illustrated in Fig 4.18, do not quite have the presence of the full unit. The arc can be divided by using a protractor, or by repeatedly bisecting the angle with the compass. These division lines represent the valleys between flutes or between peaks. In the case of the peak-and-valley variety, it is necessary to mark each division with an intermediate line for the peaks. In laying out the design on the material for fans and other incised designs of this type, it is wise to continue the lines past the planned extent of the carved area. This way, the layout lines will still be available after the wood within the area has been carved away, and can be redrawn as necessary.

To carve these designs, the perimeter is stabbed in, the central disk delineated in the same way, and the area of the rays sloped toward the disk. It is advisable to leave a small disk "covering" the point of convergence; otherwise, the narrowing flutes or peaks become too minute and are liable to crumble, which leads to an uneven appearance. In carving larger fans, the slope should be checked with a straightedge: the tendency is to work the area around the disk down to the desired depth while neglecting the center portion, thus leaving a hump. Periodically redraw the lines defining the divisions. As these lines approach the disk they come closer together, allowing a visual check on their evenness.

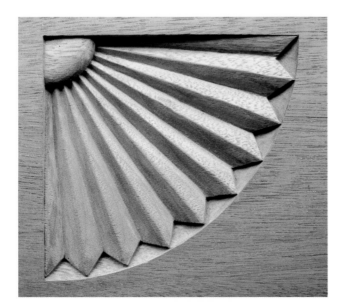

Fig 4.18 A corner fan of peaks and valleys, with half-units at the sides

In the practice exercise at the beginning of this chapter the flute was laid out across the grain. This makes carving the straight sides easier, because the grain is consistent. In radiating flutes, however, the grain is not so congenial. It is prudent to start by making a shallow cut in the middle of the flute area, which helps you to "read" the grain: one side of the gouge will be cutting against the grain in some flutes, parallel or perpendicular to it in others.

The ends of the flutes should be set in first. To make a clean end wall, a round-nosed chisel can be used: this is simply a modified bench chisel with its tip ground in a semicircle. (Incidentally, this tool is also helpful in carving the internal corners or coves of Gothic tracery.) At the inner, disk end, the flute can be finished by a small #11 modified gouge, ground so that the wings are set back from the middle of the sweep. This allows the leading bottom edge to contact the disk first, and prevents the wings from marring the wall of the disk.

To start the flute, a gouge narrower than the width of the flute is best, reversing the direction of cut as necessary to achieve the desired width. The same progression of gouge widths as in the exercise is used. Ideally, the flute should be semicircular in section: the depth is half the width. Work toward the ends, setting in with the round-nosed chisel as needed to obtain the depth desired.

The peak-and-valley type of fan is approached in the same way as the vertical body of a letter: a stop-cut is stabbed along the center of the valley first, then the sides are worked down with a paring chisel—I use a modified fishtail chisel, ground with one side beveled and the other flat, like a regular bench chisel. The idea is to get sharp lines at both valleys and peaks, with planes at about 90° to each other. In some examples the valley is closer to one peak than the other, which creates a louver-like appearance. In the example of Fig 4.18 the profile of the ends echoes the section, and lends some visual interest to the geometric arc.

CARVING A FAN WITH INFILLED FLUTES

Though fans are not often embellished, the one illustrated in the following sequence of photographs—a commission for a ceremonial chair—has many geometric additions (Fig 4.19). A similar fan is discussed in Chapter 7 (pages 145–8). The chair fan is flat, and applied to the structure of the chair. It is composed of two main levels: the flutes on the outer perimeter and the projecting reeds in the inner area. They are separated by fillets and hemispherical beads which create additional levels. In the center is an applied quarter-sphere to create added depth.

Fig 4.19 An ecclesiastical
chair back with a fan
consisting of reeds, flutes,
fillets, and beads. Note the
carved finial at the top (by
courtesy of First Presbyterian
Church, Rocky Mount, NC)

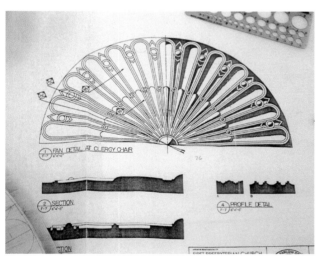

Fig 4.20 Drawing of the chair-back fan, with shading and
sections (by courtesy of Terry Byrd Eason)

Layout has to be carefully done and the various levels understood before work begins. Note in Fig 4.20 that the elevation drawing has a shaded portion and that several sections are given across as well as along the flutes. In order to delineate these levels clearly, different-colored pencils can be used to mark each area. For the sake of efficiency, and to determine the various levels, a router fitted with a ¼in (6mm) straight bit is used. This defines both shape and depth simultaneously (Fig 4.21).

USING THE ROUTER

A few notes on freehand routing may be in order at this point. A router with pear-shaped handles mounted low on the machine allows you to place the heels of your hands on the surface to be routed, affording good control. It is advisable to rout across the grain as much as possible but, of course, a large percentage of this project involves

Fig 4.21 The levels of the fan
set down with the router

diagonal grain, so use a sharp bit. It is best to rout the center of the recess first and then shave to the line. You may want to stay back from the line slightly to allow for paring the walls with a chisel, especially if the grain prevents you from obtaining a straight edge. It should not have to be said that you must use the appropriate safety wear. It is possible to rout the flutes in part by using a corebox bit with a rounded bottom, but there are several dangers in doing so. The flutes become deeper as they become broader, so it should be obvious that the bit will not create the entire shape desired. Realistically, it is as quick to carve the flutes by hand.

A lip is routed around the semicircular blank so that it fits into the structural frame (as with any raised panel). For this operation the router is mounted on a long, narrow piece of plywood, with a hole drilled at the appropriate radius and located over a pin at the center point of the blank (see page 144 and Fig 7.8). The second level is then routed in order to outline the silhouette of the fan. Routing the lowest level first gives the router more surface on which to rest, and ensures that guidelines are not cut away. It is, as a corollary, efficient to clean up the vertical walls as you rout each layer. The third level up is that of the fillets which separate the flutes. Because the surface of the flute borders is below the inner semicircle of reeds (which is the fourth level and the original surface of the blank), the entire area of the flutes can be routed. There is a lot of potential for error, and for chip-out in such areas as the hemispherical beads. Fig 4.22 shows the blank routed and the hemispheres carved.

Begin carving by cleaning up the overall outline of the shape, making sure the flutes are semicircular and the peaks between them are even. Next, round over the larger beads: this prevents them being split off inadvertently

Fig 4.23 A detail of the finished fan, showing the flat bands or fillets around the beads

while working on other areas. Much of the work in this fan is in cleaning along the straight lines, and the best tool is a paring chisel. Using a fairly wide chisel should give smoother transitions between the overlapping cuts. The idea is to work the lowest areas first: the upper areas may become damaged but, provided a little extra material has been left from the routing, they can be carved cleanly in their turn.

The narrow flutes and the fillets around the large beads and peaks should be done next. Then the large flutes are deepened, starting with a stop-cut at the end of the reed. The reeds are then rounded over to a semicircular section; note how they stop so as to leave a semicircular area at the center. Finally, a shallow semicircular block is glued onto the surface of the blank at the convergence point. Fig 4.23 shows a detail of the completed fan.

CARVING THE SUNBURST

Like the fan, the sunburst consists of flutes, or peaks and valleys, or entirely of reeds. The difference is that the sunburst is round or elliptical. The design can be incised into the surface of the material or carved separately and let into a recess. To draw the circular version, the circle is simply divided into an equal number of degrees; the widths of the divisions of the perimeter (their chords) are equal as well. As with fans, it is difficult to maintain the regularity of the elements as they diminish in width, so a central disk is commonly used.

The ellipse is a little tricky because it is made up of two different arcs, which vary depending upon the measurements of the major (longer) and minor (shorter) axes. One method of drawing an ellipse when one knows the minor axis dimension is to use two equilateral triangles (Fig 4.24a). Draw a straight line to represent the minor

Fig 4.22 The routed blank, with the hemispherical beads rounded over

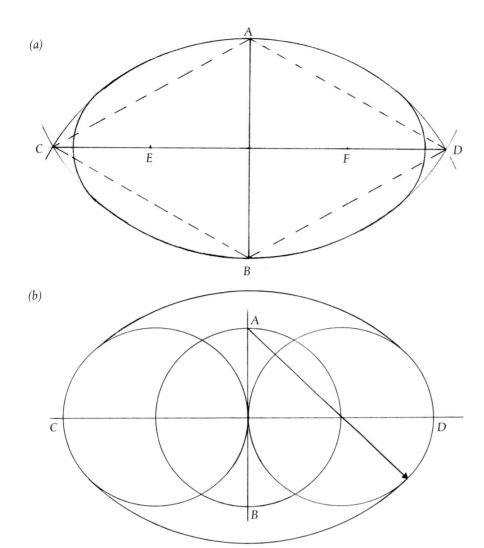

Fig 4.24 Drawing the ellipse:
(a) the use of equilateral
triangles when the required
width is known
(b) The use of three circles
when the required length
is known

axis (the vertical line in Fig 4.24a). Set your compass to this known dimension and, placing the fixed leg on the line at A, draw a semicircle. Replace the fixed leg at the point where this arc intersects the vertical line (point B), and again draw a semicircle, creating the vesica piscis shape ADBC. Connect the four points ABCD to create two equilateral triangles, with a common base on the minor axis. Bisect the altitudes of these two triangles to give the points E and F. Use these two points as centers for the ends of the ellipse, adjusting the compass until the arc is tangential to the larger arcs of the vesica piscis. (These end arcs do not extend to the apexes of the triangles.)

Another method can be used when the desired length of the major axis is known (Fig 4.24b). Draw a straight line and mark on it the overall length CD. Bisect this line and raise a perpendicular as before, then bisect the two segments so as to divide the overall length of the major axis into four parts. At the three internal points draw

three overlapping circles: the circumference of the middle circle cuts the perpendicular at A and B, and passes through the centers of the outer two circles; the outer circles pass through the end points of the axis. With center A, draw a large arc which meets the two outer circles at a tangent; repeat on the other side of the figure, with center B. The straight line drawn from A, through the center of the outer circle, indicates where the circle and the large arc merge.

One may have to suit the shape of the ellipse to the available space. This is easily done by simply changing the relationship of major to minor axis. Retaining the length of the minor axis, the ellipse can be made rounder by placing the centers for the end arcs (points E and F) closer to the intersection of the axes. Of course, the closer they are to the intersection, the closer to a circle the figure becomes. On the other hand, as one moves the centers towards the apex of the vesica piscis, the smaller the arcs (circles), and the more pointed the figure becomes. The same applies when the length of the major axis is known: as the centers of the end arcs move toward the axis intersection they become larger (the radius becoming longer) and overlap. As the centers move outward and become smaller, the ellipse becomes narrower. Adjustments will have to be made to the centers on the minor axis to complete the figure.

Fig 4.25 A small sunburst being carved in a routed recess. The center disk is being rounded over

Fig 4.26 The parting tool being used to define the valleys between the reeds of a double sunburst

To mark out the flutes or reeds, it is not sufficient simply to pick a measurement and step off the increments around the perimeter, or to give each division the same number of degrees. This will look uneven, because the ends of the flute or reed are cut off nearly perpendicularly at the axes, but obliquely between the axes. Also, the flutes or reeds near the major axis will appear narrower than those near the minor axis (in spite of the fact that the center disk is also an ellipse). Personal preference may require that the major and minor axes be the centerline of reeds or flutes (as opposed to valleys, which would be an

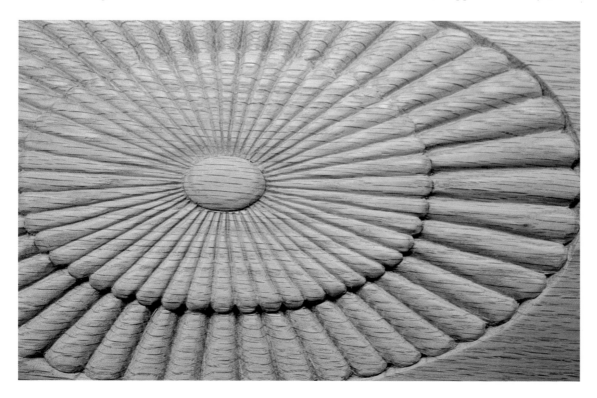

Fig 4.27 Detail of double sunburst

easier layout). Instead of bogging down in mathematical calculations, lightly sketching the increments of one quadrant will help you to determine how many increments fit well into the space. Some adjustment should be made so that all elements appear to be the same width at the perimeter. Sometimes, of course, the increments are so small that these issues are hardly troubling.

When transferring the design to the blank, I usually draw the ellipse directly onto the material. It is hard to trace an ellipse through carbon paper accurately. Plastic templates for this purpose can be purchased, but the largest are only 3–4in (75–100mm) in length.

The small sunburst being carved in Fig 4.25 illustrates the method of using a routed recess to secure the blank. It also shows how the surface is sloped in toward the center

disk, the same as for a fan. For larger applied sunbursts, the waste from bandsawing the blank can be used to hold the work. This piece can be snugged up to the blank and nailed to a scrap backing board in order to hold the blank while carving. The holding pieces may need to be made thinner than the blank in order to give access to the edges of the carving.

Fig 4.26 shows the parting tool being used to carve the valleys between reeds of a double sunburst. Fig 4.27 shows a detail of the finished piece; Fig 4.28 shows it used (with flanking vertical sunbursts) on a mantelpiece.

The variation in Fig 4.29 shows the ends of the reeds sloped, which adds some visual interest by creating a pseudo-scalloped edge. Sometimes the ends are literally concave, as in Fig 4.30.

Fig 4.28 The double sunburst in position on the central frieze block of a mantel. Two vertically oriented sunburst designs appear on the pilasters (by courtesy of Steven and Chloe Raynor, and R. L. Seiler of Buck Island Builders, Charlottesville, VA)

Fig 4.29 A variation in which the reed ends are sloped to create the feel of a scalloped edge; carved and let into a recess

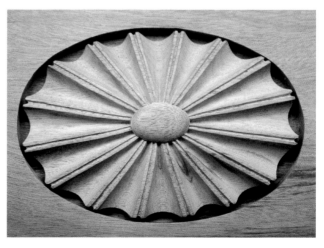

Fig 4.30 A further variation, again set into a recess, in which the flute ends are concave

CARVING THE SHELL

The shells most often used for ornamental purposes are the scallop and the cockle. The great scallop, *Pecten maximus*, the Altantic Bay scallop, *P. irradians*, and the Atlanta deep sea scallop, *P. magellanicus*, all are possible inspirations having similar characteristics. They are circular shells with 15 to 18 ribs; the convex outer (obverse) ribs are as round as the valleys between them, while the inner (reverse) surface has flatter ribs or none at all. Both obverse and reverse sides are depicted in furniture and architecture.

The cockleshell is similar but much more convex near the hinge. The common European bivalve is *Cardium edule*. The natural shape of the interior of the cockleshell lends itself to decorating the head of a semicircular niche.

Other species of mollusks may also be stylized, but not nearly to the same extent as these two. A notable naturalistic depiction of various shells is Grinling Gibbons's Kirtlington panel (private collection, Great Britain), in which a lobster and a crab dangle with fowl and fish.

Though the scallop has undulating or wavy elements, the concave and convex shapes on both interior and exterior present different decorative uses. The exterior is most often an applied ornament and presented by itself, as on a chair apron or cresting. The interior, on the other hand, provokes a wider array of decorative uses, often in association with foliage, ribbons, garlands, and cornucopias (Fig 4.31). Somewhere during the decorative evolution of the shell interior, the hinge curled into a volute. I am not aware of any bivalve mollusk having this particular feature, but snails (gastropods) and the nautilus do have shells which, as a whole, spiral about themselves. It may have seemed logical to blend the two types of shells. At any rate, the carved scallop and cockle often contain matched volutes. The scallop is a strictly symmetrical form and has the same attraction as the fan and other radiant forms.

THE OBVERSE SHELL

The carved version of the obverse scallop tends to be flatter than the natural form, though the idea is to emphasize the undulation of the surface as well as the expanding (radiating) lines. The outline can be a simple arc or more elliptical. The number of undulations may depend on the species of wood used, the size of the piece, and the configuration. Regularity and symmetry, as well as a gentle flow of line, are necessary to make a pleasing ornament.

To draw the scallop shell, describe a circle with a compass. Through the center draw perpendicular lines (Fig 4.32a). Though the natural scallop has 15 to 18 ribs, these may prove to be too small to carve well (as with the diminishing rays of the fan seen earlier), or may be appear too busy or too delicate to be effective aesthetically. In this example there are nine convex ribs.

The perimeter of the circle can be divided by quickly sketching the rays, but the divisions need to be regularized by some convenient method. A convex rib should end with a convex silhouette or outline, and one of these should straddle the centerline; otherwise, the top will look flat. In our example there are three and a half divisions per quadrant (that is, the centerline and three additional ribs), with a fourth below the horizontal diameter as shown in Fig 4.32a. The extent of the "hump" is denoted by two divisions below the diameter. Draw an inner circle to indicate the limits of the undulations of the perimeter: this will be helpful in sketching these alternating arcs. The horizontal hinge sweeps in from the

Fig 4.31 Shell associated with cornucopias, Verona, Italy

(a)

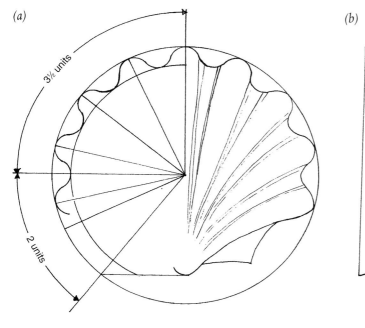

3½ units

2 units

(b)

Fig 4.32 Drawing the obverse scallop shell:
(a) The process of dividing the circle and producing the undulating edge
(b) Cross section of the shell, showing the pronounced hump towards the hinge
(c) Shaded drawing of the completed shell

(c)

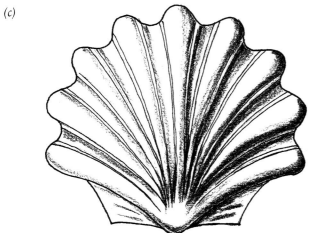

protruding hump. The basic form, with its convexities smoothly blending into flutes, does not necessarily provide enough definition, so fillets are often used to interrupt these undulations. This can be seen on the right side of Fig 4.32a, and in Fig 4.32c. Note that the outline of the shell has uninterrupted undulations, while the surface has the combination of rib and fillet (compare the finished carving in Fig 4.36).

What is important at this stage is the accuracy of the perimeter increments. The drawing of the ribs need not be precise, because the entire surface will be carved, so these lines will need to be re-sketched by hand later. As the undulations become smaller toward the hinge, there is some difficulty in keeping them separate. Even on the surface of natural shells, the divisions merge into one another (the successive coatings of calcium, like coats of paint, fill in the valleys), so some simplification is practical. If you plan to include fillets, they should fade into the flutes so there is only a series of grooves at the hinge edge, fading into a smooth hump. It may be advisable to draw a section along the centerline to see how the hump rises quickly at the hinge side and then recedes in a smooth curve to the outer edge (Figs 4.32b and 4.33). The high point (the most projection) occurs at a little less than one third of the length from the hinge.

Fig 4.33 An edge-on view of the shell, showing the lowered hinge and the curve of the shell from "hump" to edges

CARVING THE OBVERSE SHELL

After transferring the design to the blank, bandsaw the overall circular perimeter, the hinge, and the lower projection of the "hump". If the shell is large enough for the perimeter undulations to be accurately bandsawn, by all means cut them. On small shells the undulations can be defined by paring the edge with gouges. It may be helpful to transfer the division or undulation marks to the edge of the blank to aid in this carving.

The blank is then mounted on a backing board by screws through the board and into the back of the shell. If you don't feel confident in this method, use the method of gluing the shell to the backing board using several layers of newspaper and water-soluble glue. If quite small, the shell blank can be held in a routed recess with double-sided tape, like other small blanks. Mount the hinge so that it will point toward you once the backing board has been clamped to the bench.

Define the wings of the hinge with a parting tool and take these areas down close to the backing board. You can either define the perimeter profile first and then shape the surface curve, or vice versa. There may be some reassurance in having the outline complete before modeling begins. This is fine if the profile has been accurately cut, but most likely some rectification will be necessary. If the first option is to be followed, be careful to keep the edge walls perpendicular to the back surface; otherwise the outline will vary from the top surface layout, and you may produce a lopsided shell. Match the proper tool to the curves and pare down to the backing board, being

mindful of tear-out at the back. Grain tear-out while paring is more likely to occur at the top of the shell than at the sides.

Begin curving the surface from the perimeter edge, and increase the length of cut while working back toward the "hump". Cuts diagonally to the grain prove to be the most efficient, as we are creating a compound curve: along the centerline, and from side to side across the width of the shell. A large flat gouge, a #2 or #3, is probably the best choice; turned over, it can fair in the cuts for a smooth surface. Switch hands, and use the heel of the hand as a pivot. This shaping can be done quickly. The perimeter should be left about ⅛in (3mm) thick. The "hump" is close to the hinge edge, so the curve is much steeper on that side. Without removing the shell from the backing board, sight parallel to it in order to check the symmetry of the side-to-side curve as well as the centerline profile (Fig 4.33). When you are satisfied that the form has smooth curves, the centerline can be marked across the top from the lines remaining on the edge. A flexible plastic straightedge is useful for this. The undulation or division marks should also still be visible on the edges. Draw the dividing lines, from the perimeter to the center point on the hump. The smoother the blank, the easier it is to draw accurate lines.

The convex rays are defined with a parting tool, and the areas between them cut down with a small flat gouge. The rays are rounded from the perimeter to the projection of the "hump"; the cross section should match the perimeter silhouette. After rounding the convexities—

Fig 4.34 The shell partially carved; the areas of fillet and flute have been lowered, and the convexities on the left have been rounded

being careful not to dig into the flat area—the flutes are sunk into the flat area (Figs 4.34 and 4.35). There is no need to redraw the flute, as one can begin lightly in the middle and adjust while working it down. The flutes are carved all the way down the curve to the waste board.

It is not necessary to be too fussy in carrying the elements completely to the hinge-side edge, but again, regularity is important. The hinges should have some modeling, as the plain flat surfaces attract attention otherwise. A few passes with a moderate sweep will do. The completed shell is shown in Fig 4.36.

Fig 4.36 *The completed obverse shell ready for application to a flat ground*

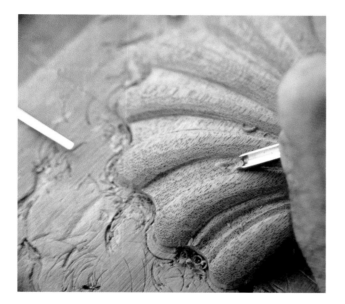

Fig 4.35 *Carving the flute, leaving fillets either side*

The exterior shells of the Goddard-Townsend block-front chest and of some tall-case clocks are treated the same way as above, though often they have more relief, surmounting as they do raised panels. The raised panel and the shell can be isolated by routing away their respective backgrounds. Though the section through the shell is somewhat different from the exterior shell described above, the approach is the same. Fig 4.37 shows the progressive stages in carving this type of shell.

Fig 4.37 *A block-front shell for the door of a tall-case clock, showing progressive stages of carving*

THE REVERSE SHELL

Most versions of the reverse or interior shell have volutes to define the hinge, often very fanciful or sprouting foliage, as in our example. From very shallow, below-surface shells (Fig 4.38) to niches, the reverse shell has been extremely popular.

To carve this shell, first isolate the volutes and leaves by lowering the area where the shell itself will be (Fig 4.39). Do the preliminary modeling of the leaves and join them smoothly to the volutes. Carve the volutes as described on pages 73–5, then attend to the interior of the shell. Dish the surface and carve the flutes (Fig 4.40). I left the fillets between the flutes fairly broad so that I could carve a fine secondary flute down the middle of each one. Pare the outside perimeter and complete the foliage. Cut the shell from the excess material and back-cut the edge of the shell. The completed piece, suitable for a cresting or pediment, is shown in Fig 4.41.

Fig 4.38 *A shallow below-surface shell with gilded finish*

Fig 4.39 *Isolating the volutes and foliage of the reverse or concave shell*

Fig 4.40 *The concave shell carved and the perimeter silhouette pared*

Fig 4.41 *The completed ornament*

5

KEYSTONES

Astragal-and-cyma profile • Scrolled • Relief

The reader may not have thought of keystones as an outlet for his or her talents, but there is a wide range of possibilities, from the precisely geometric to the excitingly bizarre. True, the keystone would not be found separated from an architectural or furniture context (except as a paperweight, perhaps), but in my career I have carved quite a few. As mentioned in the Introduction, carving such geometric millwork is one aspect of the trade carver's repertoire, requiring accuracy to maintain symmetry. Keystones are also a good vehicle to carry relief carvings of symbols and other images.

The arch, used extensively by the Romans of the Imperial period (though not unknown to the Greeks) and succeeding epochs, is a construction which allows for an open span to be "bridged" using separate blocks of stone or bricks. This is an improvement over the limited and inflexible post-and-lintel (**trabeation**) system used in Greek temples, since stone has very little tensile strength, but considerable resistance to compression. The trapezoid-shaped blocks or bricks of an arch are called **voussoirs**. The central voussoir, the **keystone,** is often emphasized for decorative purposes.

The arch has been adapted to many different situations and so, too, have decorative keystones. They are found over arched doors and windows, gateways, and niches. There are only rare examples of the keystone employed on furniture, and these are of an architectonic nature, as would be expected. In Renaissance Mannerism the keystone was adapted to decorate horizontal lintels, which do not logically require them. A drawing in Sir Banister Fletcher's *History of Architecture on the Comparative Method* illustrates 35 variations of the arch. There are,

> We should remember that even Nature's inadvertence has its own charm, its own attractiveness.
>
> MARCUS AURELIUS, MEDITATIONS

however, various pointed and multi-centered arches which do not lend themselves to emphasized keystones. From classical times the keystone took on significance, as it represents the locking mechanism of the arch, and was therefore considered a special element to be enlarged and decorated. The keystone was often decorated at entrances and gateways with symbols of protection, welcome, and industry, as well as identification.

All keystones, by function, have a trapezoidal or wedge shape. The sloped sides are on the radii of the semicircular arch and should, when extended, intersect with the center of the arch. The arch starts at the horizontal **spring line** (or **springing line**), which in the case of the semicircular arch coincides with the diameter. This line also represents the division between arch and the **impost**, which is often emphasized with mouldings (Fig 5.1). The keystone shape will depend upon the number of voussoirs, the actual dimensions of the arch, its curvature (whether true semicircle or segment of a circle), and whether the keystone extends below the adjacent voussoirs. The sides do not deviate from parallelism more than 5–10°.

For the carver, there are generally three types of decorated keystones: those which are scrolled (very much like a console bracket), those whose trapezoidal shape serves as a background for relief carving, and those whose face or front elevation is profiled with central astragal and flanking cyma or reversing curves. In woodwork the keystone is purely decorative and has no structural function; in most situations it is associated with moulded trim around the arch. This trim or facing is called the **archivolt**, corresponding to the **architrave** around a

Fig 5.1 The arcade of the West Range at the University of Virginia, Charlottesville, showing prominent keystones and projecting brick imposts

rectangular opening. The outside of this moulding (or of the voussoirs themselves) is called the **extrados**, while the interior is the **intrados**. Most keystones project above the extrados, but some drop below the intrados. In the case of a vault, the intrados is sometimes coffered, as can be seen on the Arch of Titus in Fig 5.16 (page 109).

ASTRAGAL-AND-CYMA KEYSTONE

Carving the astragal-and-cyma keystone, though it is not as common as the scrolled keystone demonstrated below, is a good introduction to "geometric" carving. By this I mean that the forms are shapes which can be expressed geometrically and without direct reference to nature. In addition to its functional trapezoidal elevation, the keystone usually has a sloping front face with profiles carved into it (Fig 5.2). The front slopes from its greatest projection at the top to its least at the bottom, making the face of the keystone more visible to the viewer below the arch. The archivolt mouldings (if any) usually butt onto the sides of the keystone. In designing the keystone, enough thickness, front to back, must be allowed for these mouldings. Because keystones diminish in width, top to bottom, the profiles on the face do the same (Fig 5.3), and this is the challenge in carving this type of keystone. These tapering profiles cannot be achieved with conventional machinery.

Some renditions have a valley between the astragal and each cyma (as described below), but more depth can be obtained if there is a flat-bottomed or "sunken" fillet between the elements, as shown in the drawing and succeeding explanation. The profiles wrap around to the top and bottom surfaces, which, being parallel, can be machined.

THE BLANK

There are several ways to fabricate a blank for this keystone, and depending upon one's situation the sequence may vary. Mark vertical centerlines around the blank, and mark the slope of the front on the sides. Throughout this book I mention the need for layout lines: I don't mean to reduce carving to a robotic exercise, but having some guidance instills confidence and, certainly in geometric elements such as keystones, they are required for

Fig 5.2 The profiled keystone on a window arch in combination with side lights, making a Venetian, Serlian, or (especially in American terminology) Palladian window; Alexandria, VA

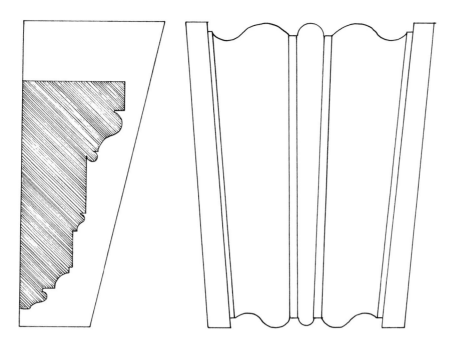

Fig 5.3 Drawing of the front and side elevations, showing the astragal and cyma profiles; the shaded area represents a possible archivolt section

accuracy. At the risk of redundancy, it is better to use layout, patterns, and jigs than to be frustrated with an asymmetrical or out-of-balance result. With practice (especially doing multiples), familiarity may allow you to eliminate some lines, relying instead on tool choice and machine set-ups. The most efficient method of producing this variety of keystone would be to grind knives for a shaper (spindle moulder) in order to cut the top and bottom profiles. Then one would connect the two by carving the diminishing profiles on the front face. Knives are ground for only one half of the profile, as the blank is flipped for the completion of the symmetrical profile. This operation is done before the sides and front are cut.

Partial machining can be done on a table saw with a regular saw blade. The sunken fillets and the raised border can be sawn on the top and bottom of the blank.

Because the border fillet on the front face is parallel to the sloping sides, this can also be defined by machine after the sides have been cut. Use a miter fence or jig to cut the angled sides of the keystone. In order to cut the sloped front face on the bandsaw, one piece of waste should be taped back onto the blank. Depending upon the accuracy of the machining, a hand plane may be needed to dress the face to the layout lines. It is conceivable that, if the sunken fillets between astragal and cyma are wide enough for a saw blade, these could be cut on the table saw as well. The sunken fillets on the face are deeper at the top than the bottom, so check the set-up before sawing. These fillets are not parallel to the side face, so some adjustment of the fence would have to be made, using an angled spacer. Fig 5.4 shows the blank with top and bottom partially machined.

Fig 5.4 Astragal and cyma keystone with top and bottom surfaces machined on the table saw. The bordering fillets and the sunken fillet either side of the center bead have been defined

Fig 5.5 As an alternative to machining, the sunken fillets are handsawn. Note that because the blanks are wedge-shaped, it is easier to clamp them in pairs in the vise

If the use of the table saw is not possible, a handsaw can be used to establish the depth and placement of the various elements, as shown in Fig 5.5. Alternatively, a chisel could be used to set in the straight lines and a narrow chisel to excavate the sunken fillets or steps.

A pattern can be made to mark the curves of the top and bottom profiles on the back of the blank. Once the depths of the steps and sunken fillets have been determined, however, it is simply a matter of rounding over and grooving the profile—which, after some practice, can be done by eye.

If two keystones on opposite sides of an opening are to be connected along the intrados, the side edges of the connecting board should have the same angle as the keystone to which it joins. The profile on the bottom of the keystone is carried along the surface of this board to connect with the second keystone. Again, if the top and bottom are to be run on the shaper, this piece can also be run at the same time.

CARVING THE MOULDINGS

It is logical to begin with the straight profiles of the top and bottom (if not previously machined), and then proceed to the diminishing profiles of the front face. For two or more blanks, the two sloping sides can be matched by turning one upside down and then clamping the pair in the bench vise, as in Fig 5.5. A rubber pad between them will prevent them from slipping and will protect

their faces. Begin by carving the sunken fillets to establish the location of the center astragal. Clean out between the saw kerfs with a narrow chisel. Round the astragal and the shoulders of the cyma to either side, using the #5 or #7 gouge turned bevel-up as in Fig 5.6.

Fig 5.6 Rounding the top profiles, with the gouge bevel-side up

Fig 5.7 The completed top profile

Fig 5.8 Using the backbent gouge to round the astragal

Next, determine where the concave portion will begin, by marking the small step next to the bordering fillet. With a deep gouge (#8 or #9), begin the groove a little inside the step. It will become apparent that the wall between the concave and convex areas requires paring so that the gouge can continue to complete the groove. With a shallow gouge fair the two curves; check by sighting from the back of the blank. Fig 5.7 shows the completed top surface.

For the front face, the procedure is the same. It is hard to work the entire length with the same gouges, however, as one has to work with the grain—that is, down the slope. A backbent gouge is used to round over the center astragal as well as the convex part of the cyma profiles (Fig 5.8). The deep gouges used for the top and the bottom concavities should be supplemented by one of an averaged width, as in the exercise described on page 85 (Fig 5.9). The first part of the concavity can be carved with the larger gouge; switch to the medium gouge about a third of the way down the blank, and finish with the smallest. It takes a little practice to fair the diminishing groove. One way to achieve this is to use the wing or side of the gouges. Periodically smooth the transition between concavity and convexity with a shallow gouge (Fig 5.10).

Fig 5.9 *The three different widths of #9 gouge used to carve the diminishing concavity on the face of the keystone*

Fig 5.10 *Using a shallow gouge to smooth the transition of the cyma profile*

Fig 5.11 *Using a round file to smooth the concavity. Note the flat bastard file used to even the sunken fillets*

Fig 5.12 The completed astragal and cyma keystone in tulip poplar (Liriodendron tulipifera)

After reasonable effort to smooth the surfaces with gouges, files are used to smooth any slight irregularities remaining (Fig 5.11). The completed keystone is shown in Fig 5.12.

USING RASPS, FILES, AND ABRASIVES

Files can produce a very smooth finish, and sanding is nearly eliminated, but it must be cautioned that one should not rely upon rasps and files to do the shaping. Some may argue that using files and rasps is an attempt to correct sloppy carving technique; but they definitely have their place in producing geometric millwork. Of course, moulding planes, scrapers, and such tools should be used when possible: they are more easily controlled than carving gouges. In instances where such tools cannot achieve the intended result, files are a very reasonable alternative and certainly better than sandpaper, if only because they do not leave grit in the wood fibers, which would dull your tools in any subsequent carving.

There are many different kinds of files, each of which is suited for work in a particular material. Those which a woodcarver would use are limited in number, however.

There are four factors to take into account when describing a particular file: cut, coarseness, shape (cross section), and length.

- *Cut* describes the arrangement of the teeth on the metal blank. *Single-cut* files have a series of parallel ridges or blades (if you will) at an oblique angle to the long edge. These files are used for abrading metals. *Double-cut* files have a second set of parallel ridges intersecting the first, which separates the first ridges into individual teeth. Providing more clearance, this cut is used for the removal of softer materials such as wood. The teeth of the *rasp cut* are freestanding with plenty of space around each, which prevents clogging when working fibrous materials.
- *Coarseness* naturally refers to the size of the teeth: there are three grades, *bastard*, *second-cut*, and *smooth*. The teeth of each grade are sized in proportion to the length of the file. This becomes complicated, as there is overlap. For instance, a bastard 10in (255mm) file will have coarser teeth than a bastard 6in (150mm) file, while a long, fine-grade file will have the same-sized teeth as a shorter, coarser file: 10in (255m) smooth equals 8in (200mm) bastard.
- *Shapes* include flat, half-round, round, triangular, and square. There are also many specialty files in a multitude of sections.
- *Lengths* are usually standardized in 2in (approximately 50mm) increments.

However, there is always the need for a smooth surface in producing millwork, so sanding may be essential. Carve cleanly and completely before sanding. Determine which areas require sanding and which can or should be left: geometric shapes, flat surfaces, straight lines will all need to be accurate and smooth, while naturalistic foliage can be minimally softened with fine steel wool. To preserve sharp arrises, sand concave surfaces and curves first, then sand the flat surfaces. This way the edges which have inadvertently been abraded are made crisp again. It is often worth a little effort to make sanding blocks which match the profile to be sanded. There are many shapes available in rubber and other materials from woodworking supply houses, but many shapes can also be shop-made from scrap wood, dowels, and cork. A stiff or brass-bristled brush in conjunction with blowing through a straw can be used to free chips and fuzz. A flap sander can be used to gently round forms, but its use should be limited as too much rounding destroys crispness. I have recently been using fine steel wool (grade 0000) after the final sanding.

SCROLLED KEYSTONE

The scrolled keystone is similar to the scrolled or voluted bracket in that it has two connecting volutes on each side, which determine the undulating front profile. Note the similarity of the two forms in Fig 5.13, which shows two corbels at the imposts of the arch and a matching keystone (shown in detail in Fig 5.14). The wedge shape of the keystone in front elevation is maintained, however. Many scrolled keystones have projecting eyes to the side volutes, as seen in Fig 5.15. Also in this example, the front face has profiles comprising a center astragal, flanking cymas and bordering fillets, as described above. The keystone on the Arch of Titus (82 CE) shows highly embellished side volutes (Fig 5.16). It also has a statue of Rome personified perched on the bottom **baluster** or roll. Along with the nearly ubiquitous acanthus leaf (Figs 5. 17 and 5.18), garlands may drape from side to side (Fig 5.19), and there are combinations of scales, flutes, beads, and leaves (Fig 5.20).

In the example described here, the volutes basically form an inclined plane (Fig 5.21). Other examples may be somewhat more elaborate, but the front elevation always takes precedence, as the projecting spirals add interest to the otherwise familiar trapezoid. The volutes can be made geometrically correct, using the same method as for Ionic capitals. (Suitable methods are described in my *Carving Architectural Detail in Wood*, pp. 77–9, and in the books by Palladio, Serlio, and Chitham listed in the Select Bibliography.) An easy method, however, is based on that

Fig 5.14 Detail of the scrolled keystone with foliage and baluster

Fig 5.15 Scrolled keystone with astragal and cyma profile and protruding side scrolls, Richmond, VA

Fig 5.13 Scrolled keystone and console brackets around an arched window: Federal Court Houses, Richmond, VA

Fig 5.16 Highly embellished scrolls on the Arch of Titus, Rome. Note the coffered intrados of the arch

109

Fig 5.17 *Keystone with foliage, Piazza della Repubblica, Florence, Italy*

Fig 5.18 *Keystone with acanthus and leaflets perpendicular to scroll, Phoenix Club, Cincinnati, OH*

Fig 5.19 *Keystone with garland and scale diaper, Richmond, VA*

Fig 5.20 *Keystone with scale diaper, flutes, and drops, Capitol Building, Frankfort, KY*

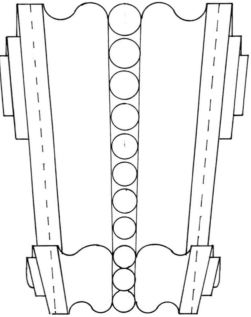

Fig 5.21 *Design for a scrolled keystone; shading on the side elevation indicates the position of the archivolt moulding*

DRAWING THE DESIGN

To draw this spiral you only need a straightedge and a compass. The diameter of each successive semicircle is three quarters of the proceeding one. Start by determining the overall diameter of the volute; mark this length AB upon a line and describe a semicircle from its center C (Fig 5. 23a). To draw the second arc, first divide the radius CB in half; this gives point D, which is where the second semicircle will terminate. The length AD is three quarters of the original diameter AB; divide this remaining segment in half to determine the next center point E (Fig 5.23b). Using this new center, adjust the compass to continue the curve on the opposite side of the line AB (Fig 5.23c). Repeat the process of finding three quarters of the diameter and marking the new center (Fig 5.23d). The construction lines become confusing, so label the centers and/or erase construction lines as you go (Fig 5.23e). Generally five or six semicircles are sufficient (Fig 5.23f). The spiral appears to lean forward somewhat, but in this application that is not undesirable.

A perpendicular line through the center C of the large volute will supply the placement of the smaller volute. The larger semicircle of the small volute is half the diameter of the large one. The first center can therefore be located by measuring up from the bottom of the blank one half the larger diameter. Connect the two volutes freehand with reversing curves; the continuing lines "die" into the other volute at the point where the second semicircle intersects the line AB. The dimensions of the blank are determined by the requirements of the trapezoidal keystone and by the thickness of the archivolt mouldings. Dotted lines on

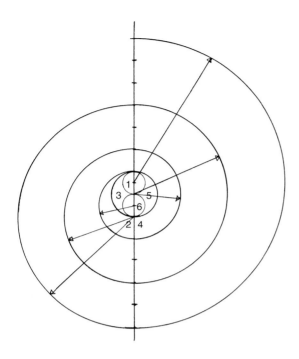

Fig 5.22 Alberti's method of drawing the volute

described by Leon Battista Alberti in his *Ten Books of Architecture*. In his method a series of decreasing semicircles are connected, the centers of each being on the same axis (Fig 5.22). The method explained below is similar but allows the spiral to decrease more rapidly. Certainly any method can be used.

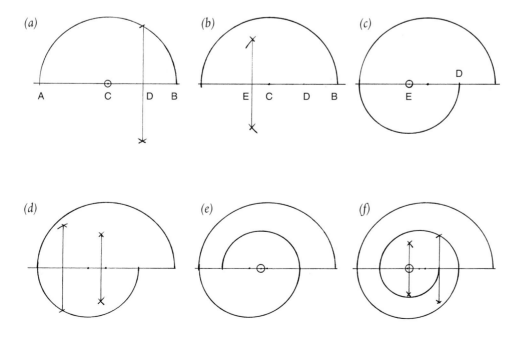

Fig 5.23 Stages in drawing the volute
(a) *The first semicircle is drawn on the baseline and the termination of the second semicircle is marked at D*
(b) *Determining the center of the second semicircle*
(c) *Drawing the second semicircle*
(d) *Steps a–c are repeated as many times as necessary*
(e) *Erase construction lines when you have finished with them*
(f) *One more arc will suffice to complete the design*

the drawing signify the basic trapezoid shape of the keystone; the blank needs to be made wider than this, to accommodate the projecting volutes as well as the connecting band between them. The scroll thus "sits" on the basic form of the keystone. The thickness of the blank from front to back should be one half the height, plus enough flat ground behind the volute to allow for the archivolt mouldings. Because these mouldings appear to go behind the scroll, it seems to be superimposed on the arch, and thus looks less obviously functional. One possible archivolt profile is represented in the shaded section on the drawing.

CARVING THE SCROLLED KEYSTONE

After striking a centerline around the blank, lay out the trapezoid shape both front and back. On the front add the allowance for the scroll width. This double marking reiterates the relationship of the scrolls to the basic form. Transfer the scrolls to both sides from the drawing, using carbon paper or photocopy and spray adhesive. Bandsaw the front profile, true up, and re-mark the deleted lines.

Begin carving the sides by bosting (isolating) the scrolls (Fig 5.24). Continuing the curve of the front profile smoothly at the top, set in the arc of the volute from front to back until it meets the band connecting the two volutes. You could continue to set in the arcs of the large volute, but then return to the inner edge of the band and continue by setting in the band and the back of the small volute. Take the ground down to the trapezoidal form using the guidelines on the back of the blank. This will take some work, as the small volute projects significantly above the ground (unless some wasting has been done already). You might wish to lower the small volute to

its intended projection while you are doing this grounding; however, this creates an uneven surface and makes the blank difficult to hold while working on the second side. The work station may accommodate the blank, but clamping in a bench vise is probably a better solution.

Begin the incline of the spiral at the eye of the large volute, working around toward the front of the blank as in Fig 5.25. Use a very shallow gouge, or, with care, a chisel. Constantly release the piece from the vise for inspection, to see that the incline is even and that successive turns are parallel. While working on the second side, compare it with the first for symmetry. At the lower end the inclined plane reverses in order to rise at the small volute; the change occurs at the back of the small volute (Fig 5.26). The thickness of the band should be consistent from the large volute to the small one. The small volute, in this example, rises at a steeper angle (Fig 5.27).

Fig 5.25 *Beginning the slope from the eye of the large volute*

Fig 5.24 *The side scroll isolated from the basic trapezoid*

Fig 5.26 *View of the back of the scrolled keystone showing the even thickness of "steps" and joining band, and the reversal of the incline behind the small volute*

Fig 5.27 Front view of the inclined volutes

Fig 5.28 Using the round-nosed chisel to connect the concave profiles where they meet behind the baluster

The front profile is carved in the same way as the previous keystone, except that there are narrow valleys instead of the sunken fillet between the elements. A round-nosed chisel helps in joining the profiles where they meet behind the baluster (Fig 5.28). The completed keystone is shown in Fig 5.29.

VARIATIONS

The astragal can be further decorated by carving beads (Fig 5.30), beads and billets, or husks, as on any astragal moulding. (The carving of these embellishments is described in my *Carving Architectural Detail in Wood*.) On some fancier versions the cyma profile is carved with leaves sprouting perpendicularly from the astragal (see Fig 5.18 on page 110). In carving the beads on the center astragal, one is confronted with grain orientation which angles from the astragal (as compared with an astragal worked on a flat piece of stock). This makes forming hemispherical beads laborious, because in rounding over the upper side of the bead one is cutting into the grain. A backbent gouge may be helpful, approaching the bead from the side. A judicious sanding smoothes the surfaces and evens the beads. The extra effort of carving these beads adds interest to the otherwise unexciting profiles.

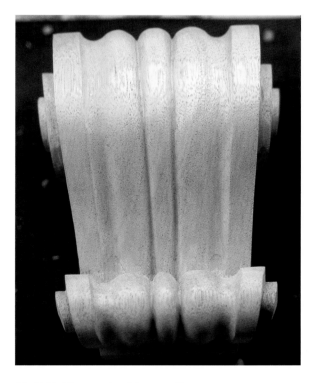

Fig 5.29 The completed front profile

Fig 5.30 A variant design with the addition of beads on the astragal section

113

KEYSTONES AS A VEHICLE FOR RELIEF CARVING

By far the most interesting variety of keystone is that which has relief carving on a trapezoidal background. It is extremely common, as it provides a basis for countless different motifs: symbols of industry like the bee of Fig 5.31, masks and grotesques as in Figs 5. 32 and 5.33, in addition to portrait heads as in Figs 5.34 and 5.35. Cherubs are shown in Figs 5.36, 5.37, and 5.38. Animals depicted are commonly lions (Fig 5.39), but also a wild boar (Fig 5.40), or even a walrus (Fig 5.41), might be a possibility! Urns and other inanimate symbols may also appear (Figs 5.42 and 5.43). Many other possibilities include heraldic devices, monograms, and cartouches (see pages 63–5 and Figs 3.9 and 3.18).

Keystones of this type may be carved in relief, or they may comprise three-dimensional carvings applied to the basic keystone-shaped background. Refer to Chapter 2 for advice on relief carving techniques.

Fig 5.31 Relief-carved bee on keystone, Rome

Fig 5.32 Grotesque mask, Vicenza, Italy

Fig 5.33 Grotesque figure with sagging teats and bat wings, Palazzo della Consulta, Rome

Fig 5.34 *Portrait head, Chelsea, London*

Fig 5.35 *Female portrait, Verona, Italy*

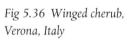

Fig 5.36 *Winged cherub, Verona, Italy*

Fig 5.37 *Cherub, St Paul's Cathedral, London*

Fig 5.38 Cherub, St Peter's, Rome (by courtesy of Kevin Maxson)

Fig 5.39 Lion, Palazzo Bevilacqua, Verona, Italy

Fig 5.40 Wild boar, University of Virginia, Charlottesville

Fig 5.41 Walrus, University of Virginia, Charlottesville

Fig 5.42 Draped urn, Alexandria, VA

Fig 5.43 Wheat sheaf, gilded, applied in a recess

TERMINATIONS

Types • Finials • Pineapple

There are several groups of ornament which can be categorized as "terminations": corbels, acroteria, terminal figures, finials, and pendants. One might include crestings, Gothic pinnacles, and symbolic objects on steeples, tombstones, staffs, or flagpoles. Many familiar terminations are carvings in the round with a sculptural quality.

Corbels are functional blocks projecting from a wall, used to support beams, arches, and label or drip mouldings over a door or window. Fig 6.1 illustrates wonderfully the comparison between the use of columns with capitals and the corbel. They are often scrolled, or formed by heads of humans, cherubs, grotesques, or animals, as shown in Fig 6.2. They are often similar to **consoles** or console brackets, but these are used to support a shelf or table and are not terminations.

Acroteria (**acroterion**, singular) are plinths or pedestals at the three angles of a classical pediment, supporting statues or other ornament. Frequently the term is used for the ornament itself when in this location. The griffin on the pediment of the Philadelphia Museum of Art (Fig 6.3) is a particularly fine example, and is used as a logo for the museum.

Terminal figures, called **terms** or **herms**, take the form of a freestanding post with a portrait bust on top (Fig 6.4). Derived from the ancient practice of using upright stones as boundary markers or milestones, many of them depict Hermes, messenger and herald to the gods, and protector of travelers. The conventionalized rendition tapers from top to bottom and sometimes has

> *Two characteristics of ornament stand out above all others. The first is its wealth, the coruscating swarm of motifs at the disposal of the artist or craftsman; the second its protean ability to change shape and dimensions whilst retaining its essential identity.*
>
> JOHN MORLEY, *THE HISTORY OF FURNITURE*

a plinth or human or animal feet at the base. Arms and torso are not usually included, though sometimes volutes decorate the sides in the manner of a scrolled bracket. A **terminus** is a figure used as a support for mantel shelves, table or tripod legs, or a corbel.

Sculptures of human figures—saints and mythological figures as well as famous personages—are found on top of many Renaissance churches, Palladian villas, and later classical revivals, as in Figs 6.5 and 6.6. They might be considered terminations, but are really more than decoration. Symbolic objects, such as the Christian cross, may also be used as terminations. The torch of Knowledge is an appropriate symbol to have atop the dome of the Jefferson Building of the Library of Congress (Fig 6.7).

FINIALS

The general term *finial* denotes a variety of forms that can be found in many architectural and furniture situations, as well as on smaller accessory items. Many terminating knobs could be included, such as drawer pulls and those on teapot lids, but the finials addressed here are those which are meant to be purely decorative. In architecture, they are regularly used to "finish off" a dome (see Fig 6.7), the piers of a balustrade (Fig 6.8), a pediment, gate and fence, or newel posts (Figs 6.9, 6.10, and 6.11). Various pieces of furniture may have finials: the pediments of high chests, desk-on-chests, and tall-case clocks particularly, but also chairs (see Fig 4.19 on page 91) and bedposts. Accessory items which are

Fig 6.1 Romanesque Revival capitals (left) and corbel, clearly showing the difference between the two. "The Castle", Smithsonian Institute, Washington, DC

often provided with finials include silverware (lidded dishes and teapots), lamps, clocks, and mirror frames (pier-glasses).

Broadly, there are two aspects of finials. First, the finial terminates a strong vertical line so that the eye is prevented from wondering off. This use of finials breaks up what might otherwise be a stark mass of building, though they are relatively small in relation to the building as a whole: they are a "crowning" ornament (see Figs 6.6 and 6.7). Secondly, some finials, due to their relationship with other architectural elements, as in pediments (Figs 6.12 and 6.13), their relative size (Fig 6.14), or their symbolic significance (Fig 6.15), cease to be merely subsidiary decorations, and become a central focus. The pineapple finial described below is a good example.

Finial shapes often derive from nature—they may depict fruits, pinecones, or foliage—or from manmade objects such as pottery and other turned forms. Fruits seem to have more symbolic value than vegetables, which are seldom used. Many finials are turned on a lathe and derive their effect from the play of concave and convex shapes and profiles. Some consist simply of combinations of these forms, without representing an actual object. The vast majority, however, have a vessel-type reference, beginning with Greco-Roman pottery.

Urns and **compotes** are larger vessels which present many opportunities for embellishment, though it must be said that mass-produced finials of smaller dimension often have the basic urn shape too. The closed form of the lidded urn copies Greek funerary urns. It usually consists of a base or foot, a small waist, the vessel itself, and a lid which often has its own knob or finial, as in Fig 6.14. The open form of the compote holds fruit, nuts, and sweets at table. The base of the compote is similar to that of the urn, while the body is wide and shallow and usually without a lid.

Fig 6.2 Corbel in the form of a bearded human head, St Paul's Onslow, Chelsea, London

Fig 6.3 Griffin as acroterion on the Philadelphia Museum of Art. Note the pendent drop between the dentils at the corner

Fig 6.4 A herm in a niche, Irwin Gardens, Columbus, IN

Fig 6.5 *Statuary atop the church of S. Vincenzo, Vicenza, Italy. Note the ornate cartouche in the pediment and the portrait keystone below*

Fig 6.7 *The torch finial on the dome of the Jefferson Building, Library of Congress, Washington, DC*

Fig 6.6 *The finials are supported by large pedestals or acroteria on Brompton Oratory, London*

Fig 6.8 *Urns terminating the vertical lines of the Corinthian columns on a steeple, Lynchburg, VA*

Fig 6.10 *Urn finial with rosettes on a gatepost, Cincinnati, OH*

Fig 6.9 *Urns terminating gateposts at "Wingate", Charlottesville, VA*

Fig 6.11 *Detail of Fig 6.9, showing fluting and flame finial*

Fig 6.12 *Urn in pediment of doorhead, near S. Maria del Carmine, Florence, Italy*

Fig 6.13 *Urn in open segmental pediment, University of Virginia, Charlottesville*

Fig 6.14 (Near right) *Large marble urn with small pineapple or pinecone finial, Albemarle County Historical Society, Charlottesville, VA*

Fig 6.15 (Far right) *Gravestone urn with leaves, Charlottesville, VA*

123

Fig 6.16 Instructions for drawing the urn in Sebastiano Serlio's Five Books of Architecture *(by courtesy of Dover Publications, Inc.)*

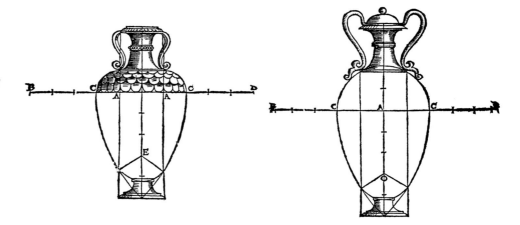

The concern for proportion among these shapes occupied Renaissance designers. Sebastiano Serlio devoted several pages of his *Five Books of Architecture* to the methods of drawing them. For instance, in one egg-shaped example (the left-hand one in Fig 6.16) he sets up a vertical centerline or axis divided into eight units, and then adds a horizontal line (up five units from the bottom) of ten units. Using a compass from one unit either side of the axis, he draws the "shoulders" of the large end of the egg. Then, with the compass set at the extremities of the horizontal cross axis, he draws the longer sweep toward the bottom. Finally, using the point on the vertical axis two units from the bottom, he draws the arc of the small end of the egg. He refers to

Fig 6.17 A collection of urn designs by James Gibbs, showing a variety of motifs including drapery, cherubs, diaper, gadrooning, and acanthus scroll (by courtesy of Dover Publications, Inc.)

the drawing accompanying the text, which shows a base about one unit high by two units wide, and a neck with handles of two units, but allows that "the rest of the workemanship shall be made according to the will and devise of the workeman" (English translation of 1584, Book I, chapter 1, folio 10). Serlio describes four different shapes, one being based on a circle. Neoclassical designers, such as Asher Benjamin in the early nineteenth century, were also concerned about the proportions of urns, and supplied directions to draw them in their pattern books. Fig 6.17 shows an array of urns designed by James Gibbs in the early eighteenth century.

One exception to the vertical orientation of finials is the decorative curtain-rod end. These can be spear points, fleurs-de-lis, ram or lion heads, foliage, palmettes (Fig 6.18), or other motifs.

Occasionally the finial form is placed in an inverted position, hanging from a ceiling or some other type of superstructure. It is then called a **pendant** or **drop**, and is commonly found on Gothic canopies, paneled ceilings, and Jacobean furniture. A pinecone pendant is sometimes found on the corners of a dentil course, filling the void created there (Figs 6.3 and 6.19).

Fig 6.19 Cone pendant in the corner of a dentil course, Richmond, VA

TURNED FINIALS

Among the many varieties of finial are those which are circular in section and begin with a lathe-turned blank. The turned finial is usually composed of alternating concave and convex shapes based on classical moulding profiles: **astragal**, **scotia**, **ovolo**, and **cyma**.

Simple turned finials can be embellished by carving these profiles with the same designs typically used on straight-run mouldings, though care must be taken because of the grain changes. An astragal ("bead" in turning parlance) can be divided into hemispherical beads (confusingly), bead-and-billet, or bead-and-reel; the ovolo can be adorned with egg-and-dart; the cyma with generic acanthus leaves, and so on. The torch in Chapter 7 (Fig 7.23, page 150) has gadrooning and a row of beads. Often the broader areas, such as the vessel body or lid, are carved with fluting (see Fig 6.11), reeding, or gadrooning. Such ornamentation, running parallel to the axis, breaks up smooth surfaces and balances the strong horizontal moulding profiles. These sorts of designs, of course, can be carved on any turned blank to be used for table pedestal, chair, candlestick, newel post, or baluster. **Reeding,** popular in neoclassical furniture, is a series of small astragals, usually with V-shaped valleys between them, rather than sunken fillets. **Flutes**, on the other hand, are long concavities, separated by fillets or flats (formed by the surface of the original blank), as on the Ionic column shaft. They are sometimes infilled (**cabled**) with bellflowers or more complicated foliage, as on the

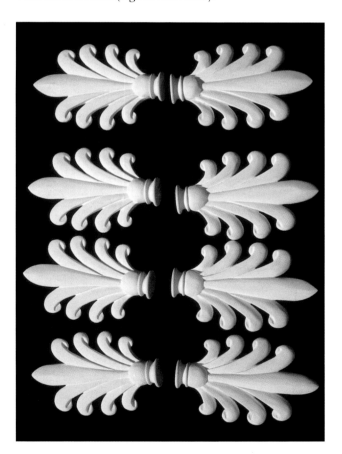

Fig 6.18 Palmette curtain-rod ends, before gilding

Fig 6.20 Urn with mask handle and gadrooning on the lower part of the body, Lynchburg, VA

mirror in Chapter 7. **Gadrooning** is similar to reeding except that the divisions are significantly larger, and projections are bulbous at the front but diminish in width as they recede, presenting a teardrop shape (Fig 6.20). The term also applies to the bulbous turnings of Tudor and Jacobean bedsteads and columns.

DESIGN CONSIDERATIONS

The size and shape of a finial are determined in part by where it will be located. In an architectural context, it is often above the viewer, so some elongation might be needed to counter foreshortening. On furniture—a high chest, for instance—the finial is close to the viewer, so this consideration is not as important. Finials remain an important aspect of furniture design, however. The architectural finial is relatively small in relation to the building, while the finial on a piece of furniture is proportionately larger and therefore takes on more visual importance. Long, shallow vertical profiles appear to have more "lift", strength, or tension, while rounder, more bulbous curves have a more flaccid or sedentary appearance. Context may determine what shapes are most pleasing. The finial should not seem to jeopardize the stability of its support by being too large or top-heavy, nor should it appear ineffectually small for its position.

In designing an effective turning, one should observe the interplay between form and surface embellishment. The decoration should not obscure the underlying form, but should be integrated with it. The sizes of the individual elements (e.g. egg-and-dart, beads, drapery

swags) should be appropriate to the form and present a unified whole. Many finials, particularly urns and compotes, rest on a plinth or acroterion (see Figs 6.6 and 6.14).

In drawing the turned outline, it is advisable to include both left and right sides, though often illustrations in sourcebooks show only half the profile. Naturally it is understood that a turning has symmetrical profiles, but it is easier to comprehend the size and shape of the finished piece when the eye does not have to "fill in" the missing part. One quick way to make symmetrical measurements is to use a compass with its fixed leg on the centerline, adjust it to the drawn profile, and then turn it to the side to be drawn. Alternatively, fold the drawing along the centerline; then, by holding or taping it to a window or light-box, the other half of the silhouette can be traced. The form will appear smaller in a two-dimensional drawing than it will in the reality of three dimensions. The shapes which compose the silhouette should be clearly defined by graceful curves, sharp arrises, and fillets. You may want to measure the circumference where decoration is planned, and draw the length on paper to help you calculate the repeating elements. This is especially advisable if your lathe does not have an indexing head.

In considering the embellishment of all turned elements, one must realize that the carvings will be largely on end grain and skewed grain. Decoration which is

Fig 6.21 Urns with garlands, Lynchburg, VA. Note how the lid part is obscured because of the viewing angle, yet the elongated finial remains visible

normally perpendicular to the run of straight moulding, for instance, will, on a turned profile, be oriented parallel to the axis and therefore with the grain. A little more care is required to deal with this different grain orientation. Remember also that the surfaces which seem dominant when drawn in elevation may become distorted, or be seen in silhouette, when viewed from below. Thus the underside of the urn suddenly becomes the most visible surface. Similarly, light is most likely to be falling on the finial from above or from the side, causing the underneath and the concave areas to be in shadow. For these reasons careful attention needs to be given to the relationship between the various elements, emphasizing or even distorting certain features to compensate for the given conditions. For example, the sweeping lid of an urn is often elongated so that the swelling of the body below does not completely obscure the top of the finial (Fig 6.21).

After determining the overall dimensions required, add several inches to the blank, top and bottom, to allow for a mounting dowel at the base as well as a reasonable amount of waste at the top. Obviously, if the design calls for a point at the top, this area will have to be the last part turned, especially if carving is to be done while the piece is still on the lathe.

NOTES ON TURNING

Most carved finials can be turned between centers and require only basic knowledge of the art of woodturning. There are many books devoted specifically to the basics: *Turning Wood with Richard Raffan* (Taunton Press) is one. If you do not have ready access to a lathe, there are many turners around who would be happy to produce the desired blank. Be sure to discuss what is involved, including aspects of design, material, and cost. The architectural and furniture urns mentioned above do not require a removable lid, so there is no call for hollowing the interior. Only a few gouges are necessary for between-centers work. Beading tools may save time in some instances, but are tricky to use. It is best to turn the bead close to the finished size before truing up with these scrapers.

There are several well-known methods and/or jigs which aid in efficiently turning a number of items of the same profile: a center-marking jig, a story pole, and plywood calipers, all of which are discussed below. Blanks should be prepared on the table saw so that they are square and of the same length. If the blanks are to be removed from the lathe for carving, it is imperative to provide extra material at either end in order to hold them in clamping blocks, as described below.

To locate the center point on the ends quickly, a simple jig can be made, consisting of a board with a square recess created by four fences, with a sharpened brad exactly at the center (Fig 6.22, left). The recess can be larger than the stock, which, when placed in the recess and rotated, self-jigs against the fences. The center of the stock is then invariably over the pin. A tap on the other end will mark the center accurately.

Once the blank has been reduced to a cylinder, the elements of the turned profile can be quickly marked. If turning multiples, a lath marked by notches on the edge at the increments of the profile can be used as a "story pole". Sharpened brads at these points can be pressed lightly into the material as it rotates to make score lines.

To size diameters accurately calipers can be used, but for repeated diameters, gauges of plywood can be fabricated without fuss by drilling a hole of the diameter required and then cutting arms, tangentially to the hole, all the way to the front of the piece of plywood (Fig 6.22, right). Open-end wrenches (spanners) are commonly used for this purpose as well. Once the blank has been reduced to these basic diameters, the rest of the turning is completed by eye; after a few repetitions, one can be fairly consistent.

After turning, the blank can either be kept on the lathe for carving, or mounted in a jig for carving on the bench. A given finial may be easier one way or the other, though it is easier to lay out circumferences on the lathe by simply rotating the blank with a pencil pressed against it. The use of an indexing head in laying out longitudinal lines is explained below. Of course, if the turning has been subcontracted, one may have to devise a jig for carving on the bench. Have the turner reduce both ends of the blank to dowels of the same diameter, or ask him to leave them square. Simple V-blocks will hold the latter. For the

Fig 6.22 A centering jig with provision for three different sizes of stock, and shop-made sizing tools

former, take two thick pieces of scrap, somewhat longer than the largest diameter of the turning, and drill holes to fit the dowels formed at either end of the turned blank. Saw each block in half through the center of the hole. Use one half of each block as a cradle or pillow block, and place the other on top as a clamping block. The removal of material by the saw blade causes the dowel ends to be held tightly when the assembly is clamped to the bench (Fig 6.23; see also Fig 7.21 on page 148). The disadvantage is that the clamp must be loosened each time the blank needs to be revolved. You may decide to make a number of these blocks so that several finials can be carved simultaneously—working all the pieces in rotation helps to ensure consistency.

A more permanent holding device, and one which will accommodate large diameters, consists of a base with perpendicular ends which contain center points (Fig 6.24). To make this jig versatile, the base can be made in two parts connected by a sliding dovetail. One of the two bolts which form the centers is ground to a point, like the dead center of a lathe; the second is ground to a flat blade. Nuts are recessed into the end pieces and fixed

Fig 6.24 A large pineapple blank mounted in the adjustable holding device

with epoxy. A second nut or wing nut acts as a brake or lock nut. Be careful to check the immobility of the work before beginning to carve.

When carving on the lathe, a table should be close by for gouges and other paraphernalia of carving. In lieu of this, a tray as illustrated in Fig 6. 25 is easily made; this can be useful for transporting gouges from one bench to another, or simply for keeping them together on the bench. To make it, use material thick enough to accommodate grooves on one side and a dado (housing) on the other. Rout flutes on the upper side using a core-box bit or a round moulding plane, making them ⅞–1in (22–25mm) wide with a ½in (13mm) space between them. The wide dado on the underside allows the tray to sit snugly on the bed of the lathe. Around the perimeter of the top attach thin strips or laths to hold the tools in place. Stacking trays can be made by extending the sides high enough to allow the bottom of each tray to clear the gouges below.

On some finials further elements are added to the basic form: garlands and drapery often accompany urns; lion, ram, and grotesque heads are often used as

Fig 6.23 Several pineapple blanks in pillow blocks clamped to the bench ready for carving

Fig 6.25 A tray for holding gouges while working at the lathe

handles. Though some of these features could be added to a turned finial, most—especially drapery and garlands—are usually integral with the form. It is difficult to add to the rounded form of a turning. It is possible to turn a separate ring or "doughnut" which would fit over the basic form, but unless the piece is of a significant size this seems unnecessary. A blank for a lion's head, or similar isolated addition, could possibly be made concave on the table saw to conform to the turned surface, though again, the turning would have to be fairly large. A better solution might be to retain enough material while turning to allow these "irregular" forms to be carved in one piece with the basic shape.

Lay out all the necessary guidelines before beginning to carve: this ensures consistency of spacing and juxtaposition of the various elements. Flexible transparent rulers are helpful for drawing straight lines on curved surfaces, as are cloth measuring tapes (seamstresses' tapes) for measuring circumferences. A strip of cardboard can also be used as a story pole or pattern. This can be especially helpful when a number of items are to be carved. The strip is wrapped around the circumference and marked; it is then laid flat and the required increments calculated. The strip is replaced and held with masking tape while the design is transferred to the blank. This method is particularly useful in laying out repeating designs, as on embellished mouldings.

CARVING THE STYLIZED FLAME FINIAL

Many finials represent oil lamps and torches (**torchères** or **flambeaux**), often with irregular, semi-realistic flames (as in the fancy fan project, pages 148–50). Lamps and torches have been a popular motif since ancient times, symbolizing life (and, when inverted, death: Fig 6.26), enlightenment and learning, wisdom and inspiration, as well as love. They appear on gateposts and domes, as already seen in Figs 6.7 and 6.11. Fig 6.27 shows a handsome baroque example. In eighteenth-century highboys the pediment acroteria are often decorated with flaming lamps or urns. Probably more familiar, however, is the helical stylization shown full size in Fig 6.28.

This type of flame finial is usually composed of two deep flutes (sometimes only separated by a sharp arris or, as in this example, a narrow fillet) which spiral around an elongated shape, terminating in a point. In historical examples this flame is the dominant element of the finial, the urn being either rudimentary or nonexistent; it has only the slightest amount of turning at its base. Sometimes the matching flame finials on a highboy spiral in opposite directions.

Fig 6.26 *The inverted torch and laurel wreath as symbols of death, Charlottesville, VA*

Fig 6.27 *Baroque torch, Tribunale Civile e Penale, Florence, Italy*

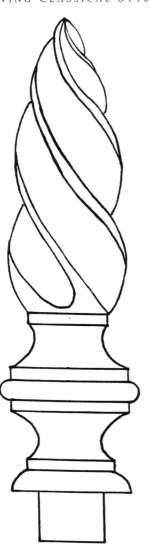

Fig 6.28 (Left) Full-size working drawing for a stylized flame finial

Fig 6.29 (Right) The helix laid out on a pair of finials

Fig 6.30 (Above) The flutes fully carved

Fig 6.31 (Right) Use rasps and files to smooth the flutes

Once the blank has been turned, lay out the helix. You may want to use a strip of flexible cardboard, but this is usually not necessary as the flame is not more than 4–5in (100–125mm) long. Divide the circumference of the flame into four parts (90° each) and begin to sketch an angled line toward the point; repeat this process at each of the four divisions (Fig 6.29). You may need to draw several lines around the circumference of the turning in order to check the spacing of the spiraling lines. They will also serve as useful references while copying the lines to another blank. Check that the ascending lines resolve pleasingly, then use them as centerlines for the carved flutes (Fig 6.30). In historical examples there is a variety of spirals, some nearly as tight as screw threads while others are looser and more suggestive of flame. Sometimes the flutes are so deeply cut that the center of the turning appears to be cut away. Round files and/or sandpaper on appropriately sized dowels are handy in smoothing the flute walls (Fig 6.31). The finished pair of finials is shown in Fig 6.32.

Fig 6.32 The completed flame finials

CARVING A LARGE PINEAPPLE FINIAL

Finials which represent fruits, such as artichokes, cones, and pineapples (Figs 6.33, 6.34, and 6.35) usually involve a series of overlapping leaves, scales, or pyramids. The overlapping leaves of the artichoke and cone are stylized to a lozenge or rhombus shape. The layout of such design features is the same as for the helical flame above, except that there are two sets of spirals intersecting in order to create pyramidal or lozenge shapes.

The pineapple has been used as a symbol for hospitality since ancient times, and has stayed in our decorative vocabulary for this reason. Originating in the Middle East, the motif has spread throughout the West in a number of decorative variations. In its three-dimensional form it is more often than not a turned finial placed either on a pedestal (Fig 6.36) or on a turned base (Fig 6.37), in an

Fig 6.35 A cone-like finial with gadrooning

Fig 6.33 The artichoke as a newel-post finial

Fig 6.34 A variation of the artichoke finial

Fig 6.36 A pineapple finial on a pedestal

131

Fig 6.39 Pineapple in an open scrolled pediment, Lynchburg, VA

Fig 6.37 A variation of the pineapple finial with beading around the turned pedestal

open pediment over a doorway (Figs 6.38 and 6.39), or on top of a gatepost—drawing attention to the welcoming areas of a property.

Like any turned carving, this large pineapple involves two distinct processes: the turning and the carving. The project could be entirely carved if you do not have access to a lathe, but it would be inefficient and tedious to do so. It would be better to have a local turner produce the blanks. For exterior carved work, use mahogany (*Swietenia*

mahogani) or similar wood. Mahogany is stable, glues and finishes well, and will hold detail. Mahogany can be obtained in thick pieces, reducing the number of glue joints required.

PREPARING THE BLANK

Even with the thick pieces of mahogany obtainable, glue-up is necessary. Working with a full-sized drawing, calculate where the joints will be, keeping in mind the necessity of balance while turning, the problems of mounting the blank on the lathe, and the required maximum and minimum diameters. Plan to make the

Fig 6.38 Pineapple as the centerpiece of an open pediment, Richmond, VA

centerline run through the middle of the central board, so that the lathe center is not on a glue joint. To help keep the weight of the block to a minimum, cut out the silhouette of the pineapple on the bandsaw. Leave both ends square and allow ½in (13mm) all around the profile. The last layers of the stack can be shorter blocks added where the largest diameter will be. Admittedly, this creates a ragged-looking block (Fig 6.40). Always use a two-part epoxy glue for exterior applications.

Provided you have the necessary training and safety equipment, you may want to use an electric chainsaw to trim the corners so that the block is roughly octagonal at the widest point. Mount it on a 6in (150mm) faceplate using heavy screws. Check to make sure the lathe is set at its slowest speed before hefting the block onto the bed of the lathe. Several scrap pieces of lumber on the bed will support the block and raise the faceplate near to the level of the drive shaft. Be sure to double-check faceplate mounting, tailstock security, and clearance. You will be surprised and humbled at the huge chunk of wood on

Fig 6.40 The blank for the large pineapple glued up and mounted on the lathe

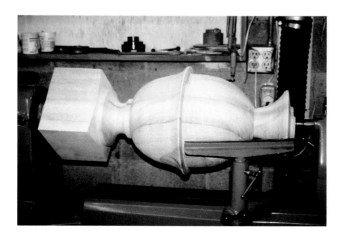

Fig 6.41 The turned blank ready for layout

the lathe. Rotate the blank by hand to test the balance. Further rounding can be done by skidding the chainsaw bar diagonally across the sharp corners.

The turning itself is fairly straightforward and uses conventional spindle-turning techniques, working from large diameters toward smaller ones. Because of the large differences between maximum and minimum diameters (14in to 5in, 355 to 125mm), lengths should be measured using a framing square with one leg against the faceplate or indexing head, and a try square. After establishing the position of the largest diameter (which coincides with the tips of the basal leaves), begin to round the block from this point, working to the right and then to the left; this will minimize vibration. Leave a fairly large section at the top end so that there is no weakness around the tail center. The top of the pineapple will be the last part to be carved before it is removed from the lathe.

In this example, the square base is integral with the pineapple, eliminating possible weather damage through a joint. The base is left oversized at first for two reasons. First, if there is any tear-out in turning the shoulder it will (hopefully) disappear as the faces are made true. Secondly, if the blank has been mounted slightly off-center, again some truing will be needed. The turned fillet just below the scotia necking is centered (since it has been turned around the center of the blank) and serves as a reference (Fig 6.41). Leaving the blank on the lathe, choose the side of the square base which is nearest this fillet and clean up with a hand plane. Check for parallelism with the bed of the lathe, by measuring the distance between the two extremes of the flat base and the lathe bed. After any necessary correction, use this face as the reference to true succeeding faces. The underside can be trued after the piece has been taken off the lathe. Because these operations are separate from the carving, they can be done before or after carving.

LAYOUT

Once the finial has been turned, lay out the carving without removing the blank from the lathe. The centerlines of the four square faces are extended along the turning to establish the 90° divisions. (An indexing head could be used to lay out the carving, but this method is just as easy.) The best way to do this is to set the toolrest at the same height as the centerline of the lathe; then rotate the blank until the centerline of each face lines up with the toolrest, and make a mark (Fig 6.42). Divide each quarter into four parts to arrive at the 16 main divisions of the carving. The toolrest can be moved along the bed to extend the lines along the turning, or a flexible ruler can be used to connect marks made at critical points (Fig 6.43). Check the accuracy of the divisions by standing at the end of the lathe and sighting down the blank. Glue lines may be distracting, so stepping around the turning with dividers will satisfy the need for accuracy (Fig 6.44). These 16 lines represent the centerlines of the large base leaves—though

you could use them to represent the spaces between them. It is easier to mark an even number of leaves than to calculate an odd number.

Sketch the tops of the large base leaves to suit the tools available (Fig 6.45). Consider the width of the leaf and the desired curve at the tip. A large #5 gouge will make a pleasing curve, revealing the secondary leaves without creating deep valleys. You may want to sketch the secondary leaves at this stage, though they will be lowered when you define the primary leaves. Strangely, acanthus leaves are sometimes carved at the base, as in Figs 6.38 and 6.46.

Fig 6.42 Marking longitudinal guidelines using the toolrest as a guide

Fig 6.45 Sketching in the base leaves

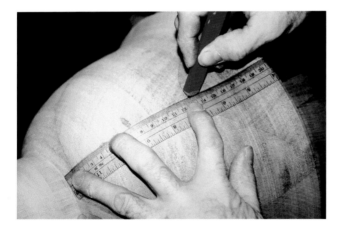

Fig 6.43 Using a flexible plastic ruler to connect lines or points

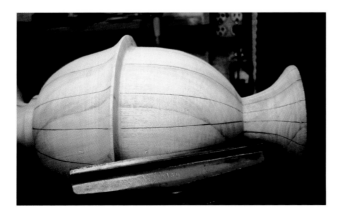

Fig 6.44 The longitudinal lines marked out along the full length

Fig 6.46 Design for a pineapple with acanthus base leaves

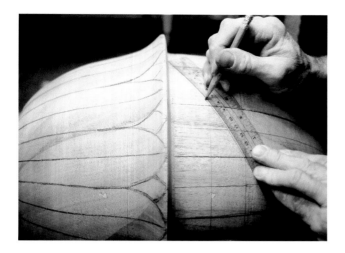

Fig 6.47 *Beginning to mark the fruit sections, using a penciled grid to ensure evenness around the form*

The fruit part should be divided into horizontal lozenge or rhombus shapes, similar to those of the natural pineapple. A pyramid whose base is a square (though often seen) gives a static effect, whereas the lozenge emphasizes the roundness of the form. In order to create these shapes, the spiral rises at an angle of approximately 35°, as opposed to 45° for a square pyramid. Starting at the top of one base leaf (and, therefore, one of the original layout lines), sketch several divisions to check the appearance. Criss-cross toward the top several times and make any necessary adjustments.

If you are fascinated by geometric relationships, you will be delighted to know that in nature the layout of divisions is not this simple, but follows a pattern known as the Fibonacci sequence. Flower petals, sunflower seedheads, artichokes, and pinecones, as well as pineapples, can all be "mapped" using this sequence. It is a numerical series in which each number is the sum of the two numbers that precede it. The series begins 1, 1, 2, 3, 5, 8, 13, 21, 34, 55, 89, and so forth. Applying the principle to pineapples, one discovers that there are invariably 8 rows of divisions sloping one way, 13 the other, and 21 vertical rows going around the fruit—all numbers of the Fibonacci sequence.

At any rate, once you are satisfied with your preliminary sketch, mark the intersections by rotating the lathe against a pencil to create a grid: your original layout lines and the newly drawn circumference lines now represent the vertical and horizontal centerlines of the lozenges. Again, a flexible ruler is helpful in extending the diagonals around the form (Fig 6.47). The measurement of succeeding rows is determined by the profile of the turning. If the diameter immediately begins decreasing, lending the fruit a pointed appearance, the lozenges will decrease more evenly. On the other hand, if the form is more rounded at the end, the divisions change quickly from nearly the same width on the parallel sides to much smaller units across the top. Near the top, some attention is required in order to keep the various lines clear; the spiral curves will need to quicken in order to retain the lozenge shape. The actual shape of the lozenge changes but, because the pineapple is seen from a low angle when mounted, these longer shapes will appear foreshortened (Fig 6.48).

Draw the top leaves in similar fashion to the base leaves—though of course they are narrower. For visual interest they could be rotated one division so that the primary leaves line up with the base secondaries.

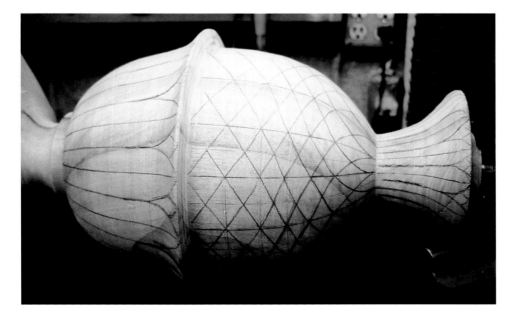

Fig 6.48 *The rhomboid sections of the fruit are fully laid out*

CARVING

Because the blank is so large, a platform can be contrived to allow you to work above it. For the setting in, the blank is held between arm and body as the gentle taps from the mallet are directed toward the internal centerline. For slicing cuts, the blank is stabilized by the locking pin on the indexing head, or by placing a combination of blocks and wedges between the blank and the lathe bed. Make sure that the work is firmly secured: in most longitudinal cutting the force is directed toward the centers of the lathe, but lateral cuts may force the blank to turn.

Set in the tips of the base leaves (Fig 6.49), then lower the area between the primary leaves, taking care to avoid breaking the leaf tips. Use a parting tool to separate the leaves, passing lightly down the line at first, then progressing deeper with subsequent passes all the way to the turned fillet at the bottom (Fig 6.50). Then define the tips of the secondaries (Fig 6. 51). With a #7 gouge, begin modeling the contours of the leaves by running a flute down each side of the centerline to create the raised

Fig 6.51 The secondary leaves are defined

Fig 6.52 The contour of the leaf is made with a #7 gouge: two grooves create a rippling effect, leaving the leaf edges and center high

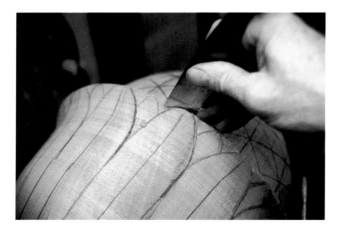

Fig 6.49 Beginning to set in the tips of the base leaves

Fig 6.50 Separating the leaves with a parting tool

central vein (Fig 6.52). Progressively smaller and quicker gouges are required as the flutes run toward the bottom (Fig 6.53). Any irregularity here can be cleaned up as the rough surfaces of the turning (visible on the vein and leaf edges) are smoothed out. For the secondaries, a simple ridge is formed by using the #7 on either side of the leaf. Fig 6.54 shows this stage completed.

To begin carving the fruit, use a medium or 60° parting tool (Pfeil #12 or Sheffield #39) to follow the penciled lines. The grain at the largest diameter may be a little tricky because of the laminations, but most of the fruit is, of course, end grain and easily worked. The wings of the parting tool are used to enlarge the valley, but a flat gouge (Pfeil #2, Sheffield #3) is needed to create apexes between the valleys; pare from the center of the lozenge shape

Fig 6.53 Leaf separation and modeling are carried down to the bottom fillet.

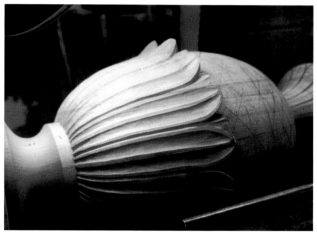

Fig 6.54 The base leaves completed

down toward the trenches to create the pyramid. Fig 6.55 shows one of the sloping sides formed, with the remaining sides yet to be done. Criss-crossing the form creates the lozenge shape. For cleaning up the bottoms of the valleys, revert to using the parting tool. Fig 6.56 shows the rhomboid-shaped fruit divisions.

The top leaves are carved in the same general fashion as the base ones. The valleys between leaf tips at the top of the blank are made shallower as they progress toward the center of the blank; this allows rainwater to drain (Figs 6.57 and 6.58). The completed pineapple, still on the lathe, is shown in Fig 6.59. This particular pineapple was flattened on the back so that when mounted against the wall it would be in three-quarter relief (Fig 6.60).

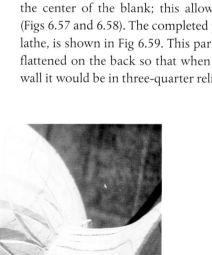

Fig 6.55 Beginning to separate the fruit sections with the parting tool; note how the spiral quickens as it approaches the upper leaves

Fig 6.56 *The completed fruit*

Fig 6.57 *The top leaves are similar to the base ones, though no attempt is made to create a center vein*

Fig 6.58 *A view of the top, showing how the leaves are separated. The shallow valleys will be continued to the center after the carving is removed from the lathe*

Fig 6.59 *The completed carving while still on the lathe*

FINISHING

Some sanding of the flat and geometric areas may be necessary, but careful manipulation of the tools and proper lighting during the process should keep such labor to a minimum. If the pineapple is to be placed outside and painted, apply a good-quality white primer. The flat finish obscures the grain pattern and emphasizes any irregularities, which can usually be corrected by a few quick strokes of sandpaper. Primer also stiffens the fuzz in the corners, which can then be removed with scraper or scrub brush.

Fig 6.60 *The pineapple completed and installed (photograph by courtesy of Phillip Beaurline)*

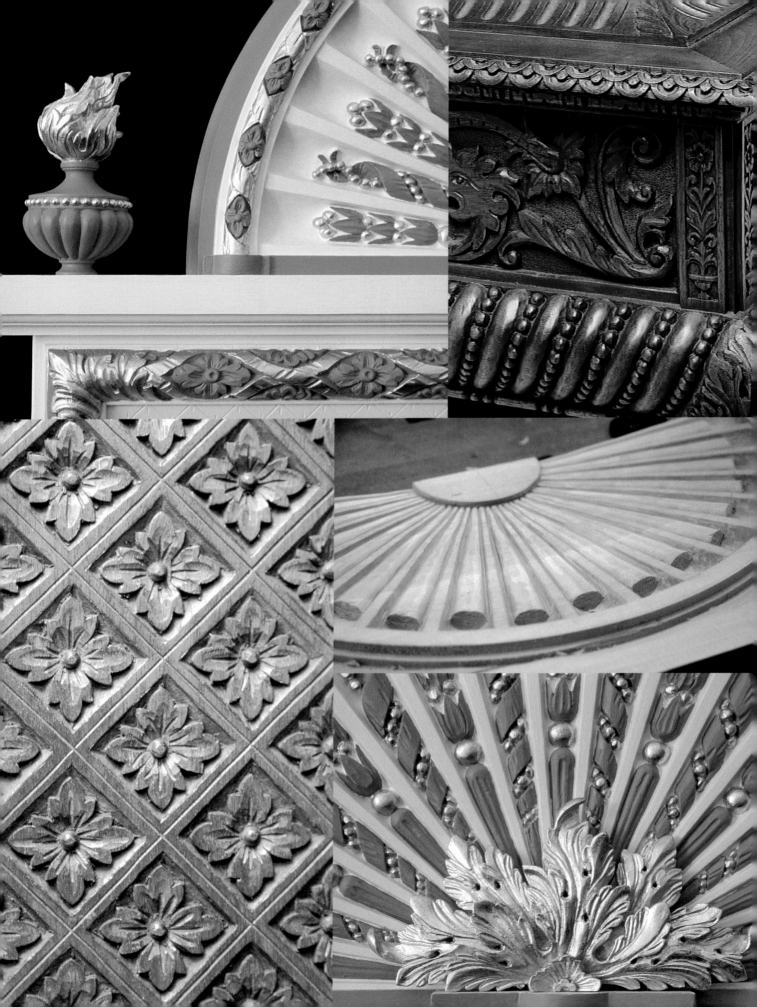

APPLICATIONS

Mirror • Cassetta

Architectural carving, by its very nature, constitutes a small portion of the overall architectural structure. It is unlikely that most readers will engage in the relatively challenging task of outfitting a room with decorative cornice mouldings and door and window architraves, or have Ionic capitals crowning pilasters—though admittedly some readers might design and carve a mantelpiece (Fig 7.1). The serious or amateur carver may be more likely to undertake the comparatively modest projects described in this chapter. These represent two significant woodcarving fields: the first is related to the picture frame; the second, carcass furniture. Of course, some of the elements discussed elsewhere in this book could be developed into viable, self-contained projects: a cartouche with name or house number is one example (Fig 7.2).

> *Design is a process, a dynamic interaction between concept and contingency, between the generic and the specific: it evolves progressively as multiple individual decisions are assimilated into the whole.*
>
> MARK WILSON JONES,
> THE PRINCIPLES OF
> ROMAN ARCHITECTURE

MIRROR FRAME

The mirror frame explained here is not directly derived from the classical orders. It does embody some of the characteristics of classicism in that the architrave supports a cornice which has a segmental pediment and acroteria; and there is an overall symmetry and order to it. In Alberti's words, "Beauty is that reasoned congruity (*concinnitas*) of all the parts within a body, so that nothing may be added, taken away or altered but for the worse" (cited in Henry Millon, *The Renaissance from Brunelleschi to Michelangelo*, p. 81). This project involves some machine fabrication, but also several different techniques of

carving. These include the incised diaper, the below-surface motifs in the flutes of the fan, the *basso-rilievo* mouldings, the applied center leaf, and lastly, the in-the-round flames of the torches.

Many traditional styles of mirror frame are of an unmistakable architectonic nature, complete with all the manifestations of the classical orders of architecture. They may have columns with capitals holding up entablatures and pediments (an **aedicule** or **tabernacle** frame) or have motifs of Greek or Roman origin. Shells, cherubs, floral garlands, voluted brackets, rosettes, and a wide variety of other designs can be found on picture and mirror frames. (See the Select Bibliography on pages 168–9 for books on the history of frames.) While shells enhanced by foliage are familiar to period-furniture makers as "high" style, the fan, being strictly geometric, is considered a vernacular decoration; but its essential simplicity allows for a variety of additional elements.

The "fancy fan" mirror frame illustrated here embodies naturalistic elements which soften the severity of the lines as well as adding visual interest. The idea, in part, comes from Grinling Gibbons's carving for the Lord Mayor's seat in St Paul's Cathedral, London, where he has used foliage to infill the flutes of a shell or fan within a niche. **Cabled fluting** is an architectural term denoting the infilling of flutes in a column or pilaster. Usually the cabling is located in the bottom third of the column and is simply a convex shape (or astragal) nestled into the flute; but it may consist of carved beading, or bellflowers, as on the iron lamp-post in Fig 7.3.

Fig 7.1 Italian Renaissance mantelpiece made from instructions and illustrations in Paul Hasluck's Manual of Traditional Wood Carving *(1911), pp. 441–7*

Fig 7.2 The cartouche described in Chapter 3 (pages 69–71) used as a house-number sign

PLANNING THE DESIGN

A scaled drawing should be made prior to the fabrication of the pieces. This will clarify your conception of the piece and help you anticipate possible problems with fabrication. Full-scale detail drawings of the fan should also be made prior to carving (Fig 7.4). In this instance a painted finish was to be used, so an elevation drawing was photocopied several times and various color combinations, including gold leaf, were tried out (Fig 7.5).

The drawing of the fan design is not complicated: semicircular mouldings define the outer border, while the center area is divided into flutes. I have experimented with different numbers of flutes and found that I prefer an odd

Fig 7.3 Cabling used on an iron lamp-post at the Philadelphia Museum of Art

Fig 7.4 Part of my working drawing of the "fancy fan", showing the cabling decorations and the central foliage overlapping them

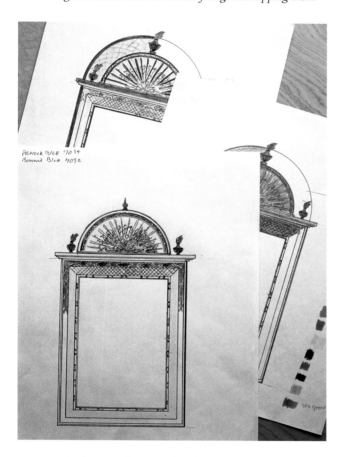

Fig 7.5 The drawing photocopied and various alternative color schemes tested

alternates a ribbon and string of pearls with bay leaves and berries. Alternating designs in this way certainly gives the fan more interest. Instead of carving the cabling in the solid, it is possible to add tapered and carved turnings to the flutes to enhance the sense of relief. Another design possibility is to alternate carved cabling with plain flutes.

There is no need to lay out the individual carvings before completing the blank, as the entire surface will be removed to leave the upstanding moulding at the edge. As always, a centerline all the way around the material is necessary. In the beginning there really is no need to lay out more than the semicircle defining the extent of the fan.

CONSTRUCTION

The foundation for this piece is, naturally enough, the frame. The basswood (*Tilia americana*) frame is shaped using the table saw, router bits, and, for the **sight-edge** bead, a combination plane (Fig 7.6). The larger moulding profile is shaped separately, using the table saw to create the fillets and hand planes to shape the half-round astragal. This and a sample bead are shown before installation

Fig 7.6 The Stanley 45 plane is used to cut the sight-edge astragal on the mirror frame

number. This means that there is a flute, infilled with carving, on the vertical centerline. Placing a plain fillet in the center would have resulted in a stricter feeling of symmetry and a less lively effect.

The cabling in the flute could be designed with a number of different motifs: wheat sheaves, torches, acanthus leaves, bundles of reeds, and so forth. This version

Fig 7.7 The foundation frame has been fabricated and assembled. A sample of the sight-edge astragal can be seen in the foreground; the large applied astragal mouldings have been carved with flower and ribbon

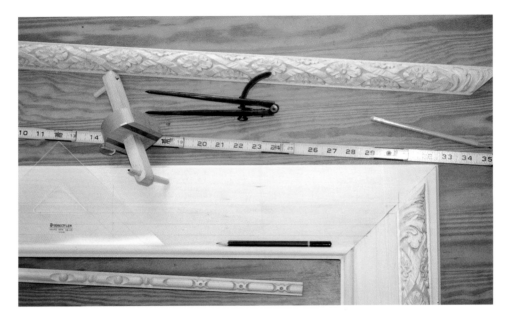

in Fig 7.7. Milling extra lengths of moulding allows you to make samples in order to work through the carving process. The frame is assembled with straight, biscuited miter joints. The moulded cornice will be biscuit-joined to the top of the frame, and the fan, fixed to a backing board, will overlap the back of both cornice and frame.

The finials are turned with a dowel at the bottom so they can be inserted into holes in the top of the cornice. The torches were turned on a lathe and the body carved while still mounted. Cherry (*Prunus serotina*) was used, as it turns and carves well.

CREATING THE FAN BLANK

The main attraction of this mirror is the fan. Start with a piece of material thick enough to provide for the sloping fluted area. The slope accomplishes two things: it brings the central applied foliage into the composition, and (since the fan will be above the viewer) it makes the sight line more perpendicular, in similar fashion to the slanted front of a keystone.

A router jig will be needed, which is nothing more than a piece of ¼in (6mm) plywood attached to the router base. A series of holes for the different radii is made at appropriate distances along the jig, just large enough to fit over the pin which serves as a pivot. This pin is fastened to a small block temporarily fixed to the edge of the blank where the center of the arc is located (Fig 7.8). A straight bit is used. Remember to measure from the correct side of the bit. The outer edge could be rough-cut on a band-saw and cleaned up with the router, but the advantage of using a router bit that does not cut through the whole thickness of the material is that the spandrel-shaped

waste pieces can serve as clamping areas. Also, given that material will be taken from only one side of the board, this extra material may help to prevent warping. Leave a little extra thickness so that the back can be trued up once the carving is complete. It is helpful to draw the intended cross section on the lower edge of the material prior to routing, as can be seen in Fig 7.8. Working inward, rout the fillets on either side of the bordering astragal. This moulding will be carved last, to reduce the risk of damage. Set the router bit to the appropriate depth to define the outer limit of the sloped fluted area.

This area should slope smoothly and evenly, as the consistency of the fillets and flutes depends on this. Because gouges are used to remove the waste material, and this tends to leave an uneven surface, some method of marking the high areas needs to be used. Simply wrapping a straightedge or block of wood with carbon

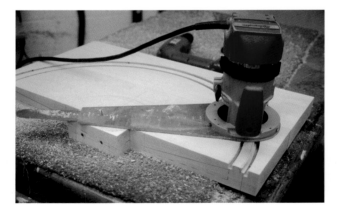

Fig 7.8 The router jig used to define the semicircular astragal which borders the fan

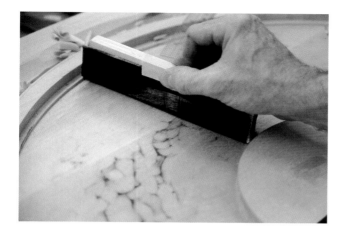

Fig 7.9 A simple method of detecting high spots is to wrap a piece of carbon paper around a straightedge and rub the surface

paper and rubbing the area as in Fig 7.9 will show these high spots. Finally, lower in several stages the central semicircle which will support the applied foliage.

CARVING THE FRAME

The ribbon-and-flower ornament is laid out and carved as described in my *Carving Architectural Detail in Wood*, starting from the center of each side and working toward the ends. The miter is "covered" by a leaf to avoid any awkwardness in turning the corner. The sight-edge bead has a simple design cut into it. Between the two mouldings is a flat (though sloping) field which has a subtle enrichment known as **diapering** (Fig 7.10). This is a wallpaper-like repeating pattern of geometric shapes seamlessly interlocking and only limited by the borders of the frame. The simplest diapers use a square grid, as here. (There is more about diapers on pages 155–7.) In this case the pattern breaks up the flat ground with slight texturing.

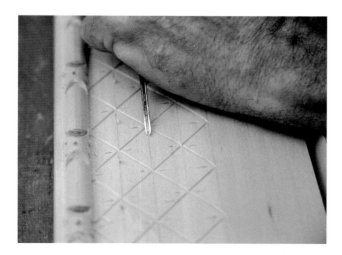

Fig 7.10 Carving the incised diaper with a parting tool

CARVING THE FAN

Lay out the centerlines of the flute divisions using the drawings as a guide; check by stepping off with a compass. Mark either side of this division the width of the flute, thus establishing the fillet width. Though some fans may look best with half-flutes at the diameter, such a layout would present awkward spaces for the carved infill. With the compass, mark the extent of the cabling. Begin carving by trenching on either side of each fillet with a parting tool. Because the wall of the flute will be almost vertical near the surface, a 60° parting tool (Pfeil #12, Sheffield #39) can be used. The larger extremity of the flute is set in with a round-nosed chisel and excavated with a frontbent #8 gouge (Fig 7.11). A frontbent #3 works well for the side walls, as shown in Fig 7.12. Care must also be taken not to pry against the flute wall while excavating the valley.

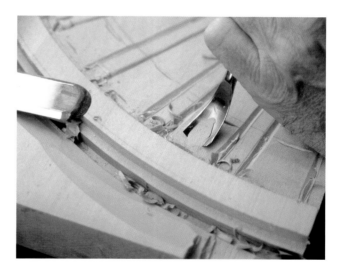

Fig 7.11 Using a frontbent #8 gouge to excavate the flute. The round-nosed chisel is used to set in the end wall

Fig 7.12 A frontbent #3 may be helpful to clean the flute wall

145

Fig 7.13 The fan blank ready for carving the decorations on the cabling

Though the cable may not be exactly semicircular, the valley between fillet and cable should be quite deep to give sufficient relief to the infill. The blank is ready for the infill carving in Fig 7.13.

Use a compass to mark the positions of the various elements of the cabling designs on each cable, then sketch the design on the convex shape. The leaf-and-berry designs begin at the large bead. It may be helpful to mark the centerline of each cable. Set in the leaves and berries, and relieve the leaves toward the berries in order to give enough depth to round the latter. A lot of clean-up will be needed in order to get the proper depth. Fig 7.14 shows the stages in carving this element. For the intervening flutes, set in the ribbon and the round area of pearls. Because grain direction changes from cable to cable, care must be taken in carving the pearls. At the end, the ribbon curls behind the string of pearls.

The applied foliage should appear generally symmetrical, but not so much as to look static. It has a rococo feel to it, and is the "playful" element of the piece. The blank is bandsawn and mounted on a plywood backing (or on the work station). Fig 7.15 shows the "levels" of leaves. After carving this piece, I realized that it did not adequately cover the inner part of the cabling, so I returned to the fan and carved another turn of the ribbon-and-pearl design (Fig 7.16).

The semicircular moulding around the perimeter of the fan is a ribbon-and-flower design—a smaller version of the moulding that surrounds the frame. Before forming the astragal profile it is best to mark the centerline, so that it can be more accurately rounded with gouges or scrapers. A backbent gouge is useful here, though an absolutely smooth semicircle is not imperative, as nearly the entire profile will be carved.

Fig 7.14 Sequence showing the carving of the laurel leaves and berries

Fig 7.15 The central foliage has been bandsawn and the first stage of differentiating the levels accomplished

Fig 7.16 The completed foliage shown in position on the finished fan

Sketch the crossing ribbons directly on the moulding (with guidance from the drawing), beginning at the middle of the top. Just a few units or increments will create the lozenge shape which will contain the flower. After determining a pleasing angle for the ribbons and a workable area for the flower, step off the increment (measured from the center of the crossed ribbons) to both ends. Make any necessary adjustments; it is best to end either side with a half-ribbon element rather than half a flower.

A SIMPLE MARKING JIG

A marking jig can be made to mark the consistent angle of the ribbon on the curved moulding. This jig is also useful in laying out rope moulding on the archivolt of a niche, for instance. The jig is made of two pieces fixed together: a curved fence or stock which rides the outside of the astragal, and a 45° angled piece which acts like the blade of a miter square.

The curved fence is made from a piece of scrap wood around 6in (150mm) long and the same thickness as the height of the astragal. Draw a line on this piece, parallel to the long side, which represents a chord of the arc of the astragal. Place it on the drawing (or on the carving itself) so that it covers a section of the astragal, and so that the line drawn on it connects two points along the arc, forming a chord of the arc. Then, using a compass or trammel set to the radius from the center of the fan to the outside edge of the astragal, draw an arc on the scrap piece, thereby replicating the arc on the outside of the astragal. (The piece will eventually be bandsawn to this line so that it will ride the astragal.) Bisect the chord

and raise a perpendicular as shown in Fig 7.17. On the perpendicular, mark the position of the centerline of the astragal; this can be seen as a dot in Fig 7.17. The 45° angle piece will need to be aligned with this mark when the two pieces are assembled.

The second part of the jig is made from similar stock (I used part of the offcut from the curved fence), with its end cut at 45°. You can obtain this angle by bisecting a right angle, or by using a protractor or a miter square. Screw this piece to the curved fence so that the 45° surface aligns with the mark on the perpendicular indicating the center of the astragal; then unscrew it, bandsaw the

Fig 7.17 The marking jig under construction, showing the layout matched to the blank underneath

curved fence to shape, and finally reattach the 45° piece. If the spiraling rope or ribbon reverses direction, as on this example, the 45° piece will have to be reversed as well, so screw it to the curved fence rather than gluing it; alternatively, it may prove easier to make a pair of jigs, or even a double-ended one. Fig 7.18 shows the jig in use.

A pattern or template can also be made and attached to a similar base fence in order to make the outline of the lozenge shape of the crossed ribbons (Fig 7.19).

FINAL CARVING

A #5 gouge defines the edges of the ribbon. There is not room enough to have an undulating ribbon edge, but a rippled surface is sufficient. Fig 7.20 illustrates the finished foliage, cabling, and perimeter moulding.

Fig 7.18 The marking piece is fixed to the curved fence so as to form a 45° angle with the radius of the fan

Fig 7.21 The torches, after turning and carving, are held in pillow blocks in order to carve the flames

Fig 7.19 A plastic (mylar) template fixed to a jig which slides along the semicircular astragal moulding

Fig 7.20 The completed fan

Fig 7.22 The completed mirror frame. (Photograph by Ron Hurst/Photoworks)

The torch flames are carved while held on the bench, clamped into pillow blocks (Fig 7.21). The challenge here is to represent the ephemeral flame in a solid material. Historically, the transient randomness has been portrayed in a variety of ways; one abstract example is the spiral finial on many eighteenth-century highboys, as demonstrated in Chapter 6 (pages 129–30). This piece adopts a somewhat more naturalistic approach.

The completed and finished mirror frame is shown in Fig 7.22, with details in Figs 7.23, 7.24, and 7.25.

Fig 7.23 Detail of the frame corner, showing the flaming torch finial

Fig 7.24 Detail showing the incised diaper, corner leaf of large astragal, and the small astragal

Fig 7.25 The gilded foliage

CASSONI

During one's career it often happens that a particular genre of carving strikes some inner chord, and for me one of those fascinations has been Italian cassoni. Though there are many pieces of Renaissance furniture surviving, **cassoni** (**cassone**, singular) or marriage chests are both numerous and enriched with a wide variety of carved ornament.

In the long history of boxes, coffers, and chests, cassoni have a fascinating story. Like the medieval coffer, these "great chests", as much as 6ft (1.8m) long, were used for the storage of clothing and personal valuables, but the cassone took on a special social significance, as many pieces of furniture do. Leon Battista Alberti, in his essay *On the Family* (*I Libri della Famiglia*, *c*.1430), uses the cassone metaphorically as "a microcosm of the household, but also, synecdochically, a figure for the wife herself" (Cristelle Louise Baskins, *Cassone Painting, Humanism, and Gender in Early Modern Italy*, p. 2). Marriage chests were symbols of social status and were lavishly decorated with carving, intarsia (inlay), and gesso relief; many were painted and gilded (some with panels by well-known artists of the day, including Uccello, Donatello, and Botticelli); and, no doubt, they were filled with expensive brocades, silk gowns, and gold jewelry. Many examples bear heraldic devices and were meant to unite families in alliances of blood and business. The genre began to develop during the fourteenth century, when the merchant and ruling classes of central Italy, particularly in the Florentine sphere of influence, acquired increasingly affluent and convenient domestic circumstances. Examples are found from Venice, and later Rome, but Florence and its artists and artisans are particularly associated with the manufacture and decoration of cassoni. "Between 1446–1465 two manufacturers alone are known to have turned out nearly two hundred separate chests for leading Florentine families, and there were about ten workshops in Florence in the first half of the fifteenth century" (Eric Mercer, *Furniture 700–1700*, p. 95). Many of these cassoni have ended up in museums around the world and can be studied first-hand.

Two influences characterize these chests: the relief frieze and the sarcophagus. Both painted and carved cassoni depict moral or profane narratives derived from the ancient Latin writers Ovid and Virgil, from the Tuscan literature of Boccaccio and Petrarch, as well as from the Bible. Often they show jousting tournaments, hunting and battle scenes, and courtship. But many are narratives about exemplary women such as Esther, Virginia, and Griselda, or heroes such as David, about the Trojan War or the labors of Hercules. Cassoni were one of the first secular art forms in the Renaissance. (In fact, there are a number of examples with a nude painted on the inside of the lid.)

Though cassoni were decorated in many different techniques, our interest is in those with relief woodcarving. As the fashion for painted walls and ceilings began to dominate the house interior, the sculptural aspects of the chests were emphasized. The overall shape changed to one with bulging sides—or at least with a prominent ovolo moulding at the base—and supported by feet. Borrowing much from the Florentine tradition, the manufacture of this type was centered in Rome. They are of the late fifteenth and sixteenth centuries. The profusion of carved detail and the narrative panels in high relief make this style of particular interest to the carver. A good example is Fig 7.26, a Venetian cassone of 1550–75.

Fig 7.26 Italian cassone showing typical form, subject matter, and treatment (Virginia Museum of Fine Arts, Richmond: Gift of Mrs E. A. Rennolds in memory of Mr and Mrs John Kerr Branch)

Beside the subsidiary mouldings—which range from geometric incised designs, through egg-and-dart to foliage and guilloche infilled with rosettes—the characteristic ovolo provides a larger profile on which to carve garlands, cherubs, and ribbon-bundled laurel leaves as well as gadrooning. In the detail (Fig 7.27) we can see that the ovolo here has a scale design in the "background", garlands in relief, and shields (trophies) between them. (Yes, there is also a nude stretched out in the middle.) The feet are often lions' paws, though some examples rest on a whole lion or on dolphins.

The principal scenes on this chest are of Neptune and Venus rising from the sea on the left, and an episode from the Trojan War on the right. Because these were marriage chests, allusions to the families participating are often present: this example has a cartouche, but no heraldic device on it (Fig 7.28). The lid on this type is derived from the "roof" of the classical sarcophagus, which has an upwardly curving moulding often carved with flutes or *imbrication*—a scale-like diaper mimicking roof tiles. At the corners are figures, grotesque mythological creatures, acanthus leaves, or cartouches (Fig 7.29). This type of chest, especially when caryatids appear at the corners, is often called a "Buontalenti" style, after the architect, engineer, painter, and designer Bernardo Buontalenti (1531–1608). These chests do not appear to have been painted, but often had gold highlights.

Fig 7.28 *Detail showing central cartouche (Virginia Museum of Fine Arts, Richmond: Gift of Mrs E. A. Rennolds in memory of Mr and Mrs John Kerr Branch)*

Fig 7.27 *Detail of the corner of the same cassone, showing ovolo at bottom, relief scene, and corner figure (Virginia Museum of Fine Arts, Richmond: Gift of Mrs E. A. Rennolds in memory of Mr and Mrs John Kerr Branch)*

Cassoni are meant to be placed against the wall, so they are long and narrow; the measurements of the chest in Fig 7.26 are 68½in long by 29in high and 23in deep (1740 × 737 × 584mm). Consequently, the artistic emphasis is on the front side. Though the ends are also decorated, and of course the mouldings wrap around the sides, the motifs usually have little to do with what is portrayed on the front, nor is the scale necessarily compatible—compare the scene in Fig 7.27 with the head on the end of the same chest (Fig 7.30).

The cassone in Fig 7.31 is a flat-topped version dating from 1525–50, though the top is not original. This example is architectonic, having pilasters supporting an entablature and arcade above. Each arch has a shell, as in a niche, with heads, possibly symbolic, in each. Cherubs smile sweetly in the spandrels of the arches. The bottom panel has typical Renaissance grotesque figures and a portrait medallion. Each pilaster with its blank medallion has a capital of foliage and what appears to be fruit, and some strange volutes. The matched panels either side of the central medallion panel are candelabra. This term describes several varieties of vertical panel which have a central axis depicting turned forms, from

Fig 7.29 *Florentine cassetta (small cassone) in walnut (by courtesy of Dover Publications, Inc.)*

Fig 7.30 *Detail of the end of the cassone in Fig 7.26, showing a head with radiating headdress (Virginia Museum of Fine Arts, Richmond: Gift of Mrs E. A. Rennolds in memory of Mr and Mrs John Kerr Branch)*

Fig 7.31 *Architectonic chest of walnut, 1525–50 (Philadelphia Museum of Art: purchased with funds contributed by Samuel W. Morris from the Edmond Foulc Collection, 1930)*

Fig 7.32 *Candelabra pilaster, showing the central "turning" accompanied by masks, animals, putti, etc.; Vicenza, Italy*

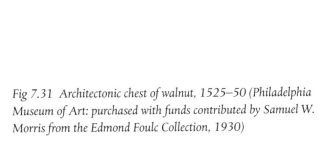

Fig 7.33 Detail of another candelabra showing mask, cornucopias, birds, and "turning"; Verona, Italy

which symmetrically flow various decorations, including tendrils with foliage and flowers, birds, grotesques, torches, and cornucopia (Figs 7.32 and 7.33; see also Figs 7.1 and 2.25, pages 142 and 40). The wall paintings of Nero's Domus Aurea (Golden House) inspired Renaissance designers, and the candelabra and grotesque became common motifs. Many of Domenico Ghirlandaio's frescos in Santa Maria Novella, Florence, are framed with such panels, and there are dozens painted on the walls of the church of S. Andrea, Mantua, designed by Leon Battista Alberti in the 1470s.

A RENAISSANCE-STYLE CASSETTA

Though the full-size cassone today may be considered a relic without contemporary context, what better way for the carver to strut his stuff than by making a toolbox as a sampler, tour de force, or "masterpiece"? The possible techniques one can use are myriad, with many decorated mouldings, relief panels, paw feet, and sculptural figures. The box described here echoes the cassone form, with similar configuration and decoration to the carved type of the sixteenth century. It is made of black walnut (*Juglans nigra*).

This chest is a double cube—twice as long as it is wide or tall, in keeping with the Renaissance fascination with such proportions. It is much smaller than the historical examples, so that it fits into my palazzo! Let's call it a **cassetta**, a small box. It is designed to contain four interior trays to hold 32 standard-sized carving gouges. The top two trays rest on a rabbet in the sides of the box, while the two below are supported by a ledger strip nailed to the interior. The space below is for storage of sharpening equipment, mallet, or clamps. A small version of the work station could be incorporated. Of course, this chest would also make an impressive jewelry box, or treasury for family heirlooms.

DESIGN OF THE CARVINGS

In addition to prodigious quantities of carved mouldings, these chests have relief-carved ends and front. My design has carved panels front and back, and diapers on the ends (where handles could be attached). The drawings in Fig 7.34 show several ideas for coffer panels, and it was the top one that inspired the front of my cassetta, but the possibilities are nearly inexhaustible. The Florentine box in Fig 7.29 shows a geometric strapwork design including cartouches, gadrooning, scrolls, and shell or fan. The small coffer in Fig 7.35 shows masks at the corners, an intricate gadroon, grotesque masks (possibly green men), and some displeased lions. On small pieces the relief is minimal, though on the large originals the relief depth can be 2–3in (50–75mm), making the walnut plank a large piece of wood.

On flat fields and borders, diapers are often used. This term, in a decorative context, means a repeated, tessellated design which can be expanded in any direction. Diapering is a surprisingly common motif, found in all the arts and crafts, though the term probably derives from the patterns of woven fabric. (It comes from the Greek *diaspros*, meaning "pure white", presumably referring to linen.) Uses range from parquetry flooring to wrought-iron grills, woven textiles, and encaustic tiles. The motif is found throughout the history of ornament, from ancient Egypt through William Morris wallpapers to contemporary quilting. The alternating black and white squares of a chessboard might be considered the simplest form; the hexagonal pattern of a honeycomb is a wonderful example from nature. Incredibly interesting, the concept

Fig 7.34 Drawings of five panels suitable for chest sides, from C. B. Griesbach, Historical Ornament: A Pictorial Archive *(by courtesy of Dover Publications, Inc.)*

Fig 7.35 (Below) A cassetta of typical cassone form with fancy gadrooned ovolo at the base, masks at the corners, and lion supporters, from Paul N. Hasluck, Manual of Traditional Wood Carving *(by courtesy of Dover Publications, Inc.)*

extends from the purely geometrical to the provocatively aesthetic. Anyone familiar with the graphic art of M. C. Escher or with patchwork quilting will be aware of the ramifications of the idea.

The units of an ornamental diaper are symmetrical, though not all units have to be the same. The structure is usually based on some sort of grid system, but, as Figs 7.36 and 7.46 illustrate, this can include curved lines and compartments of different sizes. Sometimes the geometric units contain naturalistic images, such as fleurs-de-lis, rosettes (Figs 7.37 and 7.45), or symbolic objects such as crowns, crosses, or eagles. One very good source for diaper construction and design is Franz Meyer's *Handbook*

of Ornament (reprinted by Dover Publications, Inc.); and there is a wonderful explanation for quilters in Jinny Beyer, *Designing Tessellations: The Secrets of Interlocking Patterns*. Diapers can be used in woodcarving as a subtle enrichment to flat surfaces (see Fig 7.24 on page 150)—or even curved ones, as in the case of the coffered niche in Fig 7.38—as framing compartments for other motifs, and as a foil to more salient features.

Accuracy is necessary in the laying out of diapers, in the same way that designs for chip carving need to be regular in order to be aesthetically pleasing. Sometimes there is slight modeling below the surface, as in the common design of latticework infilled with flowers (see Fig 7.37).

Fig 7.36 *A diaper design which features a curving grid and two different infill designs, from Griesbach,* Historical Ornament: A Pictorial Archive *(by courtesy of Dover Publications, Inc.)*

Fig 7.38 *Diaper, consisting of a diamond-shaped grid and rosettes, in a niche; Trevi Fountain, Rome*

Fig 7.37 *Stages in carving the diaper for one end of the cassetta, showing the geometric layout and the tools used for setting in*

The cassone in Fig 7.26 (page 151) has figures covering the corner dovetails, but my coffer has mitered corners with biscuit splines, and there was no need to cover the joint. Pilasters are often placed at the corners, so I used them at the end borders of the panels. They keep the eye from wandering off the edge, and add an architectonic feel to the box. Pilasters in architecture have the same architectural function as columns, so they need to be in proportion to the structure; but the carved pilaster panel is usually not quite as monumental. Carving candelabra panels is good practice in training the eye to assess the symmetry of your work.

CONSTRUCTING THE CASSETTA

There is nothing particularly difficult about constructing the basic box, using any of the well-known corner joints, such as the spline (biscuit) miter, the dovetail, or the finger joint. Because a number of mouldings will be wrapped around it, the box should be as square as possible. Depending upon the corner treatment, through dovetails or similar exposed joints might be covered over with a carved element. After the basic box has been assembled dry, the ledge for the top set of trays is rabbetted. The exterior panels are then carved as described below. It is wise to procure the lock, hinges, and handles before

Fig 7.39 A detail of the basso-rilievo *panel on the front of the cassetta*

Fig 7.40 The sides of the cassetta are carved and ready to assemble; some of the biscuits reinforcing the miter joints can be seen

construction—particularly the lock, to ensure that there is enough thickness to accommodate it. Make sure the key has a long enough shank to penetrate the moulding and still engage the lock mechanism.

Once the sides have been carved, the basic box is assembled (Figs 7.39 and 7.40). Then fabricate and miter the various mouldings. In this case the bottom bead-and-billet was made with a router bit and carved separately from the gadroon above it. The stock for the gadroon is cut to rectangular dimensions and the intended profile is drawn on the ends. Use the table saw to cut off waste, and then a bench plane to round the profile (Fig 7.41). The gadroon is mitered, mounted on plywood to be carved, and then fastened to the box. The top moulding is also routed, using an ogee bit. The pilasters at each corner are applied. The top is made from four boards mitered and splined, then a moulding is added to raise the center panel (Fig 7.42).

In each instance, make extra lengths and carved samples, to ensure that the parts work together and that the relative proportions are successful. As we saw before, on the original cassoni the relative sizes of various elements have little direct correspondence. The pilasters at the corners of this coffer are much more delicate than the gadroon, but as on the originals, the effect is one of pleasant naïveté.

The trays can be made with simple lap butt joints, with bottoms of ⅛in (3mm) plywood, glued and nailed. Remember that the lower trays must be slightly narrower than the upper ones, so as to fit in the lower part of the box, below the rabbet.

Because I may eventually want to convert the trays to hold jewelry, I made removable inserts to hold the gouges. I used a thin piece of plywood with triangular dividers spaced to accommodate eight tools per tray. The deep red velvet is attached with spray adhesive (Figs 7.43 and 7.44).

Fig 7.41 Stages in preparing the blanks for the gadroon, showing the cardboard profile template; at right, the finished profile with the astragal attached

Fig 7.43 Tray inserts for gouges. The triangular dividers are glued to thin plywood, and spray adhesive is used to fix the velvet lining material

Fig 7.42 An end view of the blank for the top moulding as it was fabricated on the table saw. The corner leaf has been set in on the piece below

Fig 7.44 The trays filled with tools and inserted in the cassetta. The lower trays are slightly narrower than the upper ones

CARVING

The front and back panels are carved like any low-relief carving, as explained in Chapter 2. One diaper is a below-surface rosette in a square grid (Fig 7.45; see also Fig 7.37). The other end has a different diaper consisting of semi-circles enclosing fan-like leaves (Fig 7.46).

Establishing the gadroon spacing is tricky: each increment must appear to be equal, yet their shape and length change progressively. One way to approach this problem is to figure the measurements and mark them along the top, then sketch the arcs as they progress along the profile. Simply check and redraw by eye until they look correct. No doubt a computer program could be devised to plot these curves accurately, but then where is the skill, the art, the interest? As with many classical mouldings, a leaf was designed to "cover" the miter; this eliminates messy details and gives definition to the corner. In Fig 7.47 a sample carving is being tried against the end panel. For carving, mount the blanks on a piece of plywood which can be clamped to the bench or held in the vise as required (Fig 7.48).

The crown moulding at the top is an abstract of stylized foliage, though acanthus or egg-and-dart could be used as in Fig 7.31.

Fig 7.45 The diaper design on one end of the cassetta consists of a diamond grid and rosettes, with sloping ground and some modeling

Fig 7.46 The diaper on the other end consists of leaves within a grid of semicircular scales

Fig 7.47 Testing moulding samples on the end of the cassetta. The partly carved gadroon sample is mahogany

Fig 7.49 The small pilaster blanks are held to the bench with double-sided tape

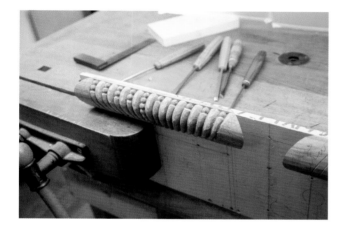

Fig 7.48 The gadroon blank screwed to a piece of plywood held in the bench vise

The pilasters can be fastened to the bench with double-sided tape, since the setting-in is perpendicular to the bench and, the grounding being very shallow, sideways pressure is slight (Fig 7.49). A completed pilaster is shown in Fig 7.50.

The top has a scale-like edge carving; Fig 7.51 shows the partially fabricated top held in a vise, assisted by a bar clamp, for carving. The corner leaves of the curved moulding are at a higher level than the fluted cove (Fig 7.52), so the entire profile needs to be lowered, first with gouges near the leaves and then with a scraper. The "thumbnail" flutes are then carved into this lowered field. Purpose-made cleats on the work station hold the piece. The partially assembled top with curved moulding in place appears in Fig 7.53.

The final step is carving the paws. Their top profiles are bandsawn, leaving the rest of the blank square so it can be held easily. They are then carved. The ogee backs of the paws are then cut on the bandsaw, and screw holes

Fig 7.50 The finished pilaster at the corner of the cassetta

161

Fig 7.51 *The top is held in the vise with the help of a pipe clamp across the bench in order to carve the edge*

Fig 7.52 *Lowering the profiled field of the curved "roof" moulding away from the corner leaf. Note the specially shaped cleat holding the mitered piece*

Fig 7.53 *The lid nearing completion*

Fig 7.54 *The completed lion feet, showing the ogee curves front and back*

drilled and countersunk. They are glued and screwed after the rest of the assembly has been accomplished (Fig 7.54). The completed cassetta is shown in Figs 7.55 and 7.56.

I finished my coffer with Minwax brand "Jacobean" stain mixed with Behlen's "medium brown walnut" filler to even out the varying colors of the wood. I then applied J. E. Moser's clear wax.

As you begin to undertake your own projects, I would hope that you have acquired a sensitivity to classical ideals and the confidence to pursue them. To be successful, you must perceive the intended carving through the understanding of process: by practicing both freehand and mechanical drawing, by developing your carving technique, and by enjoying the activity of carving as well as the end result. Accept that your first efforts will leave scope for improvement. Know that on another occasion you will face the same difficulties, but they will be easier to overcome because of your previous experience. You will eventually find the subject matter or style which excites you. It may not be a cassetta, a mirror, or a pineapple, but something appropriate to your preferences and situation. Whatever you choose, I hope this book will have helped you to acquire a vocabulary, some ideas, and a place to begin.

Fig 7.55 *The finished cassetta, front view (photograph by Ron Hurst/Photoworks)*

Fig 7.56 *The finished cassetta, back view (photograph by Ron Hurst/Photoworks)*

GLOSSARY

This list contains the definitions of words printed in bold type in the text. Please refer to Cyril M. Harris, *The Illustrated Dictionary of Historic Architecture* for additional explanations.

abacus the topmost member of a capital, which supports the architrave or beams of the superstructure of a building.

acroterion (plural **acroteria**) an ornament, often a statue, placed on a pedestal at the peak or end of a pediment; also, the pedestal itself.

addorsed arranged back to back.

aedicule (Latin *aedicula* = little house) the elements of the temple front—columns, entablature, and pediment—used to frame a niche, window, or door. **Tabernacle** also refers to this configuration, especially when describing picture and mirror frames.

affronted arranged face to face.

agrafe (agraffe) a keystone in the shape of a cartouche.

ancon a scroll-shaped bracket or console block which supports an entablature or cornice over a door or window.

anthemion a running design of stylized honeysuckle and palmettes.

Apolline the head of Apollo, the Greco-Roman sun god, depicted with rays emanating from it.

architrave the beams, resting on the columns, which form the lowest part of the classical entablature; also the rectangular surround, usually finished with mouldings, to a door or window.

archivolt the mouldings around the face of an arch, corresponding to the architrave around a rectilinear opening.

arris a corner or exterior edge made by intersecting planes or curves, as between a flute and fillet, or between two flutes as on a Doric column.

astragal a small half-round moulding, often embellished with carving.

baluster the roll on either side of an Ionic capital (front to back, between the volutes); the roll on a scrolled bracket over which an acanthus leaf is often curled.

bolection any moulding which covers a joint between pieces on different levels and projects above the surface of both pieces; often used to hold panels into a frame.

bosting (bosting-in) isolating main forms or blocking out masses as a preliminary step in carving.

bucranium (bucrania, plural) a representation of a bull's head or skull.

cabled fluting or **cabling** the infilling of flutes with a plain or ornamented astragal.

candelabra a symmetrical, vertical design in which a central member resembling a lathe-turned form sprouts foliage, masks, cornucopias, and other motifs.

cartoon a full-sized drawing of the ornamentation to be carved, used to transfer the design to the material.

cartouche a representation of a skin or parchment which curls at the extremities, often serving as a frame for an inscription; highly stylized, it can be elaborately embellished.

cassetta a small box, often of similar configuration to the full-sized cassone.

cassone (cassoni, plural) an Italian Renaissance marriage chest, often elaborately decorated.

coelanaglyphic relief another term for below-surface carving, sunken relief, Egyptian relief, or *cavo-rilievo*, in which all carving and modeling are below the surrounding surface.

coffered (of a ceiling or similar surface) divided into a regular pattern of recessed panels.

compote a vessel form, usually wider than tall, often on a pedestal base, but without a lid.

console a bracket which supports a shelf (such as a mantel) or table top (forming a **console table**).

corbel a bracket fixed to or built into a wall in order to support a beam, arch, or other structural member.

Corinthian the most ornate of the three principal classical orders, characterized by slender proportions and elaborate capitals decorated with acanthus leaves and small volutes.

crossetted (of a frame) having members which project beyond the corners, as though overlapping.

cyma a moulding of ogee or S-shaped contour.

diaper a design composed of identical elements repeating in all directions or without limit, usually based on a grid system.

Doric the most austere of the three main classical orders, distinguished by robust proportions and plain cushion-shaped capitals.

drop another name for a **pendant**.

echinus a bulging or cushion-shaped member, seen clearly in the Doric capital, below the abacus.

engaged column a column which is attached to a wall and appears to be partly embedded in it.

entablature the superstructure of horizontal members—architrave, frieze, and cornice—which rests on the columns of a building.

escutcheon a (usually) lozenge or square shape upon which is displayed a heraldic device; also a protective plate around a keyhole.

extrados the exterior extent of an arch or vault; the outside line of the voussoirs.

fan a geometric design of radiating elements, semicircular or less, often found at the corners and in the spandrels of furniture and architecture.

flambeau a stylized representation of a flaming torch.

flute one of a series of semicircular grooves, used on Doric and Ionic columns, fans, sunbursts, and elsewhere.

frieze the central member of the classical entablature, above the architrave and below the cornice, often with carved ornament.

frieze band a relatively broad, flat surface between mouldings on a wall, which mimics the frieze of the classical entablature; often ornamented.

gadrooning an ornament comprising a series of lobe-like shapes on a convex moulding, taking the form of sweeping teardrops.

golden ratio, golden section, or **golden mean** the division of a line or rectangle such that the smaller part is to the larger as the larger part is to the whole.

grotesque a Roman motif, rediscovered in the Renaissance, of mythological creatures amid swirling foliage.

grounding the process of smoothing the background (usually after bosting and setting-in have been accomplished) upon which the objects in relief will sit.

idiom the comprehensive vocabulary or characteristics of the artistic expression of a culture.

impost the block or course upon which an arch rests, often denoted by mouldings projecting from the wall.

intrados the interior surface of an arch or vault; the jamb of an arched opening. The intrados of a vault may sometimes be coffered.

Ionic one of the three main orders of classical architecture, having comparatively slender proportions and a distinctive capital with large paired volutes.

keystone the central voussoir of an arch, often emphasized with ornament.

linenfold panel a representation of folded cloth, usually with the overlapping material shown at both ends; a popular motif in late medieval and Renaissance Europe for wall paneling and furniture.

mannerism an architectural style of the late Renaissance, involving idiosyncratic use of classical motifs.

medallion a circular or oval tablet or plaque, often with a portrait bust, animal head, or similar isolated ornament.

metopes the flat surfaces between the triglyphs in a Doric frieze, often used as a field for carving.

modeling the final shaping of set-in forms, determining the curves, planes, and details of the objects depicted.

modillions a series of scrolled brackets supporting the overhanging element (the corona) of a cornice, especially in the Corinthian order.

order any of the major classical styles of architecture (chiefly Doric, Ionic, and Corinthian), each with its own characteristic proportions and decorative details; also, the ensemble of columns and entablature, considered as a whole.

ornament any motif used to embellish (decorate) an object or architectural element.

ovolo a convex quarter-round or quarter-elliptical moulding.

panel a flat area bordered (and often held in place) by rails and stiles.

pediment a low-pitched gable en of a roof: the triangle defined by the horizonta and raking cornices. A **segmental pediment** has a curved top.

pendant a finial oriented downward; also called a **drop**.

pilaster a column-like structure, attached to a wall rather than free-standing, which is rectangular in section but otherwise has the same features as a column of a particular order. A **half-column** or **engaged column** is similar, but rounded in section.

putto (**putti**, plural) a figure of a small, naked, usually winged boy; often interchangeable with cherub.

reeding a series of parallel or simultaneously diminishing astragals or half-rounds.

rinceau a design composed of scrolling acanthus or other vine-like foliage.

rosette a circular or oval ornament depicting a flower, sometimes with associated foliage, the elements radiating from the center.

roundel any circular plaque.

Scamozzi capital a variant of the Ionic capital in which the corners are turned outwards at 45°, and volutes are carved on all four faces rather than on the front and back faces only.

scotia a concave moulding in the form of a rounded groove, asymmetrical rather than semicircular in section.

segmental pediment a pediment (gable) whose shape is a segment of a circle.

setting-in the process of defining forms by creating a vertical wall from the surface outline to the ground; done after bosting and before modeling.

sight edge the inner edge of a picture or mirror frame.

spandrel the approximately triangular space between an arch and its rectangular surround, or between two converging arches.

spring(ing) line the horizontal line from which an arch begins to curve.

strapwork a design consisting to some degree of interlaced or overlapping bands, often used in conjunction with cartouche and other decorations; commonly associated with the panels popular in Jacobean England.

style a variation contained within an artistic idiom; a subset of a design vocabulary.

sunburst a geometric design similar to the fan, but circular or elliptical in shape.

tabernacle see **aedicule**.

tablet a flat panel with moulded frame upon which an inscription is carved.

term or **herm** a freestanding terminal figure, usually a bust, upon a tapering pedestal; in furniture, sometimes used as a pilaster or supportive console.

terminus a complete or partial human figure used as a supporting bracket (console) or corbel.

tondo (**tondi**, plural) a circular panel; or, in the case of oil painting, a circular canvas and frame.

torchère a stylized representation of a flaming torch.

trabeation the system of construction relying on a post-and-lintel configuration, as in Greek temples.

triglyph a section of a Doric frieze carved with three vertical bars, said to represent the end of a crossbeam in wooden construction.

tympanum the triangular area of a pediment, defined by cornice mouldings, upon which is found ornamentation such as statues, cartouches, shells, urns, etc.

undercutting the process by which material is carved away from behind a relief object to make it appear separate from the ground.

urn a vessel form, usually higher than wide, often on a pedestal base and with a lid.

vesica piscis the shape created by two opposing and intersecting arcs, resembling an American football or a rugby ball.

volute the spiral form associated with the Ionic capital, but also used, for example, on brackets and handrail ends.

voussoirs the wedge-shaped bricks or stones used to build an arch.

SELECT BIBLIOGRAPHY

The resurgence of interest in all things classical means that new editions, reprints, and new material are constantly being published. Dover Publications Inc. and Phaidon Press Ltd produce many fine books on architectural style. Phaidon has a Style Series whose titles include *[Robert] Adam, Art Deco, Arts and Crafts, Baroque, Chinoiserie, Elizabethan and Jacobean, Gothic, Moorish,* and *Palladian.* Much is showing up on the Internet; for example, at the time of writing the entire *Quattro Libri dell'Architettura* of Andrea Palladio can be found at: andrea.gsd.harvard.edu/Palladio/qlibri.html.

I habitually refer to Harris, Lewis & Darley, and Fletcher as architectural references; to Morley for furniture history; and to Hasluck for carving techniques and design ideas. For thousands of illustrations of classical style, refer to Griesbach, Rettlebusch, and Strange. Other useful books are cited in my *Carving Architectural Detail in Wood: The Classical Tradition* (GMC Publications, 2000).

The following books are published by Dover Publications Inc., 31 East Second Street, Mineola, NY 11501. Most are reprints of older books, including many important primary sources, and the original publication date is given in parentheses. It is hard to quantify the hours I have spent studying Dover reprints, or to qualify the amazing service they perform in making these wonderful old texts available to us.

Ackermann, Rudolph (ed.). *Neoclassical Ornamental Designs.* (1817) 1996.

Alberti, Leon Battista. *The Ten Books of Architecture: The 1755 Leoni Edition.* (1485/trans. 1755) 1986.

Cirker, Hayward and Blanche. *Monograms and Alphabetic Devices.* (1830, 1870, 1881) 1970.

Cole, Rex Vicat. *Perspective for Artists.* (1921) 1976.

Dürer, Albrecht. *Of the Just Shaping of Letters,* trans. R. T. Nichol. (1525) 1965.

Glazier, Richard. *A Manual of Historic Ornament.* (1894) 2002.

Griesbach, C. B. *Historic Ornament: A Pictorial Archive.* (n.d.) 1975.

Harris, Cyril M. *Illustrated Dictionary of Historic Architecture.* 1977.

Hasluck, Paul. (ed.). *Manual of Traditional Wood Carving.* (1911) 1971.

King, Thomas. *Neo-Classical Furniture Designs.* (1829) 1995.

Luckiesh, M. *Visual Illusions: Their Causes, Characteristics, and Applications.* (1922) 1965.

Morison, Stanley. *Pacioli's Classic Roman Alphabet* (late 15th century) 1994.

Palladio, Andrea. *The Four Books of Architecture,* ed. Isaac Ware (1570/1738) 1965.

Rettlebusch, Ernst. *Handbook of Historic Ornament.* (1937) 1996.

Ruskin, John. *The Elements of Drawing.* (1857) 1971.

Serlio, Sebastiano. *The Five Books of Architecture* (1584/trans. 1611) 1982.

Strange, Thomas Arthur. *Antique Furniture and Decorative Accessories.* (n.d.) 2000.

Syracuse Ornamental Company. *Ornamental Borders, Scrolls and Cartouches.* (1923) 1987.

Wotzkow, Helm. *The Art of Hand Lettering.* 1967.

The following have been consulted or are superb references, but represent only a smattering of the thousands of books available on these various subjects. Some of these titles may no longer be in print.

Baskins, Cristelle Louise. *Cassone Painting, Humanism, and Gender in Early Modern Italy.* Cambridge University Press, 1998.

Beyer, Jinny. *Designing Tessellations: The Secrets of Interlocking Patterns.* Chicago: Contemporary Books, 1999.

Biedermann, Hans. *Dictionary of Symbolism,* trans. James Hulbert. New York: Facts on File, 1992.

Boardman, John (ed.). *The Oxford History of Classical Art.* Oxford University Press, 1997.

Boucher, Bruce. *Andrea Palladio: The Architect in his Time.* New York: Abbeville Press, 1998.

Brolin, Brent C. *Architectural Ornament: Banishment and Return.* New York: Norton, 2000.

Canaday, John. *What is Art?* New York: Alfred A. Knopf, 1980.

Chitham, Robert. *The Classical Orders of Architecture.* New York: Rizzoli International, 1985.

Evetts, L. C. *Roman Lettering.* London: Pitman, 1955.

Fletcher, Sir Banister. *A History of Architecture on the Comparative Method*, 20th edn., ed. Dan Cruickshank and Andrew Saint. Oxford: Architectural Press, 1996.

Garrett, Wendell. *Classic America: The Federal Style and Beyond*. New York: Rizzoli, 1992.

Hall, James. *Dictionary of Subjects and Symbols in Art*. Boulder, CO: Westview Press, 1979.

Hayward, Charles H. *English Period Furniture*. London: Evans Bros., 1977.

Hodgson, Fred. *Practical Woodcarving*. Chicago: F. J. Drake, 1905; reprinted Ottawa: Algrove Publishing Ltd., 2000.

Howe, Jennifer L. (ed.). *Cincinnati Art-Carved Furniture and Interiors*. Athens, OH: Ohio University Press, 2003.

The International Cyclopedia of Monograms. Ottawa: Algrove Publishing, 1999.

Jackson, Anna, with Hinton, Morna. *The V & A Guide to Period Styles: 400 Years of British Art and Design*. London: V & A Publications, 2002.

Jones, Mark Wilson. *Principles of Roman Architecture*. New Haven, CT: Yale University Press, 2000.

Jones, Owen. *The Grammar of Ornament*. London: Dorling Kindersley, 2001.

Lewis, Phillippa, and Darley, Gillian. *Dictionary of Ornament*. London: Cameron, 1986.

Linley, David. *Classical Furniture*. New York: Harry N. Abrams, 1993.

L'Orange, H. P. *Art Forms and Civic Life in the Late Roman Empire*. Princeton, NJ: Princeton University Press, 1965 (first published in Norwegian, 1958).

Marcus Aurelius. *Meditations*, trans. Gregory Hays. New York: Modern Library, 2002.

Mercer, Eric. *Furniture 700–1700*. New York: Meredith Press, 1969.

Miller, Judith. *Classical Style*. New York: Simon Schuster, 1998.

Millon, Henry A. (ed.). *The Renaissance from Brunelleschi to Michelangelo: The Representation of Architecture*. New York: Rizzoli, 1997.

Morley, John. *The History of Furniture: Twenty-Five Centuries of Style and Design in the Western Tradition*. Boston: Little, Brown, 1999.

Murray, Peter. *The Architecture of the Italian Renaissance*. New York: Schocken/London: Thames and Hudson, 1986.

Onians, John. *Bearers of Meaning: The Classical Orders in Antiquity, the Middle Ages and the Renaissance*. Princeton, NJ: Princeton University Press, 1988.

Parissien, Steven. *Adam Style*. London: Phaidon, 1992.

Pierson, William H., Jr. *American Buildings and their Architects: The Colonial and Neo-Classical Styles*. New York: Oxford University Press, 1986.

Pye, Chris. *Woodcarving Tools, Materials & Equipment*, new edition in 2 vols. Lewes, East Sussex: GMC Publications, 2002.

Raffan, Richard. *Turning Wood with Richard Raffan*. Newtown, CT: Taunton, 1985.

Riley, Noel (ed.). *World Furniture*. London: Octopus, 1980.

Simon, Jacob. *The Art of the Picture Frame: Artists, Patrons and the Framing of Portraits in Britain*. London: National Portrait Gallery, 1996.

Sutton, Ian. *Western Architecture: From Ancient Greece to the Present*. London: Thames and Hudson, 1999.

Tadgell, Christopher. *Imperial Space* (vol . 4 of *A History of Architecture*). New York: Watson-Guptill, 1998.

Tavernor, Robert. *Palladio and Palladianism*. London: Thames and Hudson, 1991.

Teale, Edwin Way. *Thoughts of Thoreau: Selections from the Writings of Henry David Thoreau*. New York: Dodd, Mead & Co., 1962.

Wilk, Christopher (ed.). *Western Furniture: 1350 to the Present Day in the Victoria and Albert Museum, London*. London: Cross River Press, 1996.

METRIC CONVERSION TABLE

Inches to millimeters and centimeters

in	mm	cm	in	cm	in	cm
1/8	3	0.3	9	22.9	30	76.2
1/4	6	0.6	10	25.4	31	78.7
3/8	10	1.0	11	27.9	32	81.3
1/2	13	1.3	12	30.5	33	83.8
5/8	16	1.6	13	33.0	34	86.4
3/4	19	1.9	14	35.6	35	88.9
7/8	22	2.2	15	38.1	36	91.4
1	25	2.5	16	40.6	37	94.0
1 1/4	32	3.2	17	43.2	38	96.5
1 1/2	38	3.8	18	45.7	39	99.1
1 3/4	44	4.4	19	48.3	40	101.6
2	51	5.1	20	50.8	41	104.1
2 1/2	64	6.4	21	53.3	42	106.7
3	76	7.6	22	55.9	43	109.2
3 1/2	89	8.9	23	58.4	44	111.8
4	102	10.2	24	61.0	45	114.3
4 1/2	114	11.4	25	63.5	46	116.8
5	127	12.7	26	66.0	47	119.4
6	152	15.2	27	68.6	48	121.9
7	178	17.8	28	71.1	49	124.5
8	203	20.3	29	73.7	50	127.0

ABOUT THE AUTHOR

Fred Wilbur has practiced traditional decorative wood-carving for over 25 years. He continually researches the history and use of architectural ornament, and takes on prestigious and challenging commissions. He works with organ builders, church committees, architects, millwork companies, decorative arts companies, and ecclesiastical designers to create quality woodcarvings. Philosophically, he considers himself a perpetual apprentice, experimenting with new techniques and developing original designs.

He writes articles for periodicals such as *Fine Woodworking, Woodwork,* and *Woodcarving,* and has assisted in expanding the chapter on ornamental work in the Architectural Woodwork Institute's *Quality Standards* (8th edition). He is the author of *Carving Architectural Detail in Wood: The Classical Tradition* (GMC Publications).

Recently, the Cincinnati Art Museum videotaped Fred for its Cincinnati Wing, a permanent exhibition of the decorative and fine arts of Cincinnati. He replicated an oak leaf from the Emma Bepler mantelpiece discussed in this book. Home and Garden TV has also videotaped Fred carving egg-and-dart moulding for the program "Old Homes Restored".

He lives and works in the Blue Ridge Mountains of Virginia with his wife, Elizabeth, and delights in their new granddaughter.

INDEX

TITLES AVAILABLE FROM
GMC PUBLICATIONS

BOOKS

WOODCARVING

Beginning Woodcarving — *GMC Publications*
Carving Architectural Detail in Wood:
    The Classical Tradition — *Frederick Wilbur*
Carving Birds & Beasts — *GMC Publications*
Carving Classical Styles in Wood — *Frederick Wilbur*
Carving the Human Figure: Studies in Wood and Stone — *Dick Onians*
Carving Nature: Wildlife Studies in Wood — *Frank Fox-Wilson*
Celtic Carved Lovespoons: 30 Patterns — *Sharon Littley & Clive Griffin*
Decorative Woodcarving (New Edition) — *Jeremy Williams*
Elements of Woodcarving — *Chris Pye*
Figure Carving in Wood: Human and Animal Forms — *Sara Wilkinson*
Lettercarving in Wood: A Practical Course — *Chris Pye*
Relief Carving in Wood: A Practical Introduction — *Chris Pye*
Woodcarving for Beginners — *GMC Publications*
Woodcarving Made Easy — *Cynthia Rogers*
Woodcarving Tools, Materials & Equipment
    (New Edition in 2 vols.) — *Chris Pye*

WOODTURNING

Bowl Turning Techniques Masterclass — *Tony Boase*
Chris Child's Projects for Woodturners — *Chris Child*
Decorating Turned Wood: The Maker's Eye — *Liz & Michael O'Donnell*
Green Woodwork — *Mike Abbott*
A Guide to Work-Holding on the Lathe — *Fred Holder*
Keith Rowley's Woodturning Projects — *Keith Rowley*
Making Screw Threads in Wood — *Fred Holder*
Segmented Turning: A Complete Guide — *Ron Hampton*
Small and Miniature Turning: A Complete Guide — *Ron Hampton*
Turned Boxes: 50 Designs — *Chris Stott*
Turning Green Wood — *Michael O'Donnell*
Turning Pens and Pencils — *Kip Christensen & Rex Burningham*
Wood for Woodturners — *Mark Baker*
Woodturning: Forms and Materials — *John Hunnex*
Woodturning: A Foundation Course (New Edition) — *Keith Rowley*
Woodturning: A Fresh Approach — *Robert Chapman*
Woodturning: An Individual Approach — *Dave Regester*
Woodturning: A Source Book of Shapes — *John Hunnex*
Woodturning Masterclass — *Tony Boase*
Woodturning Projects: A Workshop Guide to Shapes — *Mark Baker*
Woodturning Wizardry (Revised Edition) — *David Springett*

WOODWORKING

Beginning Picture Marquetry — *Lawrence Threadgold*
Carcass Furniture — *GMC Publications*
Celtic Carved Lovespoons: 30 Patterns — *Sharon Littley & Clive Griffin*
Celtic Woodcraft — *Glenda Bennett*
Celtic Woodworking Projects — *Glenda Bennett*
Complete Woodfinishing (Revised Edition) — *Ian Hosker*
David Charlesworth's Furniture-Making Techniques — *David Charlesworth*
David Charlesworth's Furniture-Making Techniques
    – Volume 2 — *David Charlesworth*
Furniture Projects with the Router — *Kevin Ley*
Furniture Restoration (Practical Crafts) — *Kevin Jan Bonner*

Furniture Restoration: A Professional at Work — *John Lloyd*
Furniture Workshop — *Kevin Ley*
Green Woodwork — *Mike Abbott*
History of Furniture: Ancient to 19th C. — *Michael Huntley*
Intarsia: 30 Patterns for the Scrollsaw — *John Everett*
Kevin Ley's Furniture Projects — *Kevin Ley*
Making Great Furniture:
    30 Inspiring Projects from Top Makers — *GMC Publications*
Making Heirloom Boxes — *Peter Lloyd*
Making Screw Threads in Wood — *Fred Holder*
Making Woodwork Aids and Devices — *Robert Wearing*
Mastering the Router — *Ron Fox*
Oak-Framed Buildings — *Rupert Newman*
Pine Furniture Projects for the Home — *Dave Mackenzie*
Router Magic: Jigs, Fixtures and Tricks to
    Unleash your Router's Full Potential — *Bill Hylton*
Router Projects for the Home — *GMC Publications*
Router Tips & Techniques — *Robert Wearing*
Routing: A Workshop Handbook — *Anthony Bailey*
Routing for Beginners (Revised and Expanded Edition) — *Anthony Bailey*
Stickmaking: A Complete Course — *Andrew Jones & Clive George*
Stickmaking Handbook — *Andrew Jones & Clive George*
Storage Projects for the Router — *GMC Publications*
Success with Biscuit Joiners — *Anthony Bailey*
Success with Finishing — *Mark Cass*
Success with Joints — *Ralph Laughton*
Success with Routing — *Stuart Lawson*
Success with Sharpening — *Ralph Laughton*
Veneering: A Complete Course — *Ian Hosker*
Veneering Handbook — *Ian Hosker*
Wood: Identification & Use — *Terry Porter*
Woodworking Techniques and Projects — *Anthony Bailey*
Woodworking with the Router:
    Professional Router Techniques any
    Woodworker can Use — *Bill Hylton & Fred Matlack*

UPHOLSTERY

Upholstery: A Beginners' Guide — *David James*
Upholstery: A Complete Course (Revised Edition) — *David James*
Upholstery Restoration — *David James*
Upholstery Techniques & Projects — *David James*
Upholstery Tips and Hints — *David James*

DOLLS' HOUSES AND MINIATURES

1/12 Scale Character Figures for the Dolls' House — *James Carrington*
Americana in 1/12 Scale: 50 Authentic Projects
    Joanne Ogreenc & Mary Lou Santovec
The Authentic Georgian Dolls' House — *Brian Long*
The Authentic Tudor & Stuart Dolls' House — *Brian Long*
A Beginners' Guide to the Dolls' House Hobby
    (Revised Edition) — *Jean Nisbett*
The BIG Book of the Dolls' House — *Jean Nisbett*
Celtic, Medieval and Tudor Wall Hangings
    in 1/12 Scale Needlepoint — *Sandra Whitehead*
Creating Decorative Fabrics: Projects in 1/12 Scale — *Janet Storey*
Dolls' House Accessories, Fixtures and Fittings — *Andrea Barham*

CRAFTS

GARDENING

Creating Small Habitats for Wildlife in your Garden   Josie Briggs
Exotics are Easy   GMC Publications
Gardening with Hebes   Chris & Valerie Wheeler
Gardening with Shrubs   Eric Sawford
Gardening with Wild Plants   Julian Slatcher
Growing Cacti and Other Succulents in the
  Conservatory and Indoors   Shirley-Anne Bell
Growing Cacti and Other Succulents in the Garden   Shirley-Anne Bell
Growing Successful Orchids in the Greenhouse
  and Conservatory   Mark Isaac-Williams
Hardy Palms and Palm-Like Plants   Martyn Graham
Hedges: Creating Screens and Edges   Averil Bedrich
How to Attract Butterflies to your Garden   John & Maureen Tampion
Marginal Plants   Bernard Sleeman
Orchids are Easy: A Beginner's Guide to their
  Care and Cultivation   Tom Gilland
Planting Plans for Your Garden   Jenny Shukman
Sink and Container Gardening Using Dwarf
  Hardy Plants   Chris & Valerie Wheeler
The Successful Conservatory and Growing Exotic Plants   Joan Phelan
Success with Bulbs   Eric Sawford
Success with Cacti and Other Succulents   Shirley-Anne Bell
Success with Clematis   Marigold Badcock
Success with Cuttings   Chris & Valerie Wheeler
Success with Herbs   Yvonne Cuthbertson
Success with Mediterranean Gardens   Shirley-Anne Bell
Success with Seeds   Chris & Valerie Wheeler
Success with Wild Flowers and Plants   Julian Slatcher
Tropical Garden Style with Hardy Plants   Alan Hemsley
Water Garden Projects: From Groundwork
  to Planting   Roger Sweetinburgh

PHOTOGRAPHY

Close-Up on Insects   Robert Thompson
Digital Enhancement for Landscape
  Photographers   Arjan Hoogendam & Herb Parkin
Double Vision   Chris Weston & Nigel Hicks
An Essential Guide to Bird Photography   Steve Young
Field Guide to Bird Photography   Steve Young
Field Guide to Landscape Photography   Peter Watson
How to Photograph Pets   Nick Ridley
In my Mind's Eye: Seeing in Black and White   Charlie Waite

Life in the Wild: A Photographer's Year   Andy Rouse
Light in the Landscape: A Photographer's Year   Peter Watson
Photographers on Location with Charlie Waite   Charlie Waite
Photographing Wilderness   Jason Friend
Photographing your Garden   Gail Harland
Photography for the Naturalist   Mark Lucock
Photojournalism: An Essential Guide   David Herrod
Professional Landscape and Environmental Photography:
  From 35mm to Large Format   Mark Lucock
Rangefinder   Roger Hicks & Frances Schultz
Underwater Photography   Paul Kay
Where and How to Photograph Wildlife   Peter Evans
Wildlife Photography Workshops   Steve & Ann Toon

ART TECHNIQUES

Beginning Watercolours   Bee Morrison
Oil Paintings from the Landscape: A Guide for Beginners   Rachel Shirley
Oil Paintings from your Garden: A Guide for Beginners   Rachel Shirley
Painting with Watercolours: A Foundation Course   Debbie Flenley
Sketching Landscapes in Pen and Pencil   Joyce Percival

VIDEOS

Drop-in and Pinstuffed Seats   David James
Stuffover Upholstery   David James
Elliptical Turning   David Springett
Woodturning Wizardry   David Springett
Turning Between Centres: The Basics   Dennis White
Turning Bowls   Dennis White
Boxes, Goblets and Screw Threads   Dennis White
Novelties and Projects   Dennis White
Classic Profiles   Dennis White
Twists and Advanced Turning   Dennis White
Sharpening the Professional Way   Jim Kingshott
Sharpening Turning & Carving Tools   Jim Kingshott
Bowl Turning   John Jordan
Hollow Turning   John Jordan
Woodturning: A Foundation Course   Keith Rowley
Carving a Figure: The Female Form   Ray Gonzalez
The Router: A Beginner's Guide   Alan Goodsell
The Scroll Saw: A Beginner's Guide   John Burke

MAGAZINES

WOODTURNING ◆ WOODCARVING ◆ FURNITURE & CABINETMAKING
THE ROUTER ◆ NEW WOODWORKING ◆ THE DOLLS' HOUSE MAGAZINE
OUTDOOR PHOTOGRAPHY ◆ BLACK & WHITE PHOTOGRAPHY
ORGANIC LIFE ◆ KNITTING ◆ GUILD NEWS

The above represents a full list of all titles currently published or scheduled to be published.
All are available direct from the Publishers or through bookshops, newsagents and specialist retailers.
To place an order, or to obtain a complete catalogue, contact:

GMC Publications
Castle Place, 166 High Street, Lewes, East Sussex BN7 1XU United Kingdom
Tel: 01273 488005 Fax: 01273 402866   E-mail: pubs@thegmcgroup.com
Website: www.gmcbooks.com

Orders by credit card are accepted